The Other Days

living with a brain tumour diagnosis

Gillian Lee

The Other Days

Published by The Conrad Press in the United Kingdom 2018

Tel: +44(0)1227 472 874
www.theconradpress.com
info@theconradpress.com

ISBN 978-1-911546-28-3

Typesetting and Cover Design by:
Charlotte Mouncey, www.bookstyle.co.uk

The Conrad Press logo was designed by Maria Priestley.

Printed and bound in Great Britain by Clays Ltd, Elcograf S.p.A.

Charlie Brown: 'Some day we will all die, Snoopy.'

Snoopy: 'True, but on all the other days we will not.'

Charles M. Schulz

Several people I know have stopped putting off doing something they really wanted to do, or stopped putting off not going to somewhere they really wanted to go to. They said it was because of me and they call it: *The Gilly Factor*.

Contents

Contents

Introductions...

My family and several of my friends appear in this book. I thought it would be helpful to list the members of my family here. They are:

- my mother and father: Susannah (Gogo) and Arthur (Grandpa)

- my three sisters: Caroline, Jacky and Cecelia

- my husband Christian

- my four children: Cal, Kitty, Jens and Robin

- Baloo: our faithful family chocolate Labrador

Preface

Strangely, a few months before my diagnosis, I'd read a book by Dr Henry Marsh - *Do No Harm: stories of life, death and brain surgery* (2014) about his experiences as a neurosurgeon. The title of his book is the first Hippocratic oath in Greek medical texts. I read Dr Marsh's book without the slightest inkling that I would soon be having brain surgery myself.

The very first paragraph of 'Akinetic Mutism', which is Chapter Nineteen of his book, reads as follows:

Neuroscience tells us that it is highly improbable that we have souls, as everything we think and feel is no more or no less than the electrochemical chatter of our nerve cells. Our sense of self, our feelings and our thoughts, our love for others, our hopes and ambitions, our hates and fears all die when our brains die. Many people deeply resent this view of things, which not only deprives us of life after death but also seems to downgrade thought to mere electrochemistry and reduces us to mere automata, to machines. Such people are profoundly mistaken, since what it really does is upgrade matter into something infinitely mysterious that we do not understand. There are one hundred billion nerve cells in our brains. Does each one have a fragment of consciousness within it? How many nerve cells do we require to be conscious or to feel pain? Or does consciousness and thought reside in the electrochemical impulses that join these billions of cells together? Is a snail aware? Does it feel pain when you crush it underfoot? Nobody knows.

It's clear from Dr Marsh's book that *he* has a soul; he is a deeply sensitive man and a brilliant surgeon, and he is greatly troubled by knowing that for all his years of training and his skills, he hasn't been able to save the lives of all his patients. Also some of his patients were left brain-damaged and now exist in a mental twilight.

All of us are grateful for modern medical science and I would have died soon after my diagnosis if I hadn't been operated on. But I feel very strongly that people do have a soul, maybe not a soul that can be identified by science and put into a test-tube; but the reality of life is that we humans, and all the other creatures with whom we share our world, amount to infinitely more than the physical, biological components of our bodies.

The soul is independent of our physical substance just as the physical colours and canvas of a great painting can be said to be independent of the emotional and dramatic effect the painting produces on us, and just as the wood and catgut of a violin can be said to be independent of the effect its music produces on us.

The great writer Henry James, reviewing, in 1873, George Eliot's novel *Middlemarch* (1872), has no disagreement with the concept of a soul. James, writing at a time when next to nothing scientific was known about the human brain and how it worked, takes for granted the 'immortality of the soul', and acknowledges he does not understand the process that created the effect.

To render the expression of a soul requires a cunning hand; but we seem to look straight into the unfathomable eyes of the beautiful spirit of Dorothea Brooke. She exhales a sort of aroma of spiritual sweetness, and we believe in her as in a woman we might providentially meet some fine day when we should find ourselves doubting of the immortality of the soul.

I didn't ever imagine I'd write *The Other Days*, because I never imagined I'd contract a brain tumour. It's the sort of thing that only happens to other people, it doesn't happen to you. I wrote some chapters of this book in hospital, as a reply to Henry Marsh's musings on the soul, because I felt he didn't go deeply enough or far enough. I wrote other chapters later, but I've given this book an approximately chronological structure.

So here's my story: what happened when I was diagnosed with a stage four, glioblastoma multiforme tumour, incurable and deadly with a very short life prognosis.

And yet I saw silver linings.

The Other Days is dedicated with warm, abundant thanks to the wonderful, committed people I have met within the NHS and to my family and friends, who have all played their parts and made my role the easier for it. But for all of them it would have been a very lonely - and terribly frightening - path to tread.

1

TURNING ON A SIXPENCE

*One day she finally grasped that unexpected things were
always going to happen in life and she realised the only
control she had was how she chose to handle them. So
she made the decision to survive using courage, humour
and grace. She was queen of her own life and
the choice was hers.*

Lupthya Hermin

*Sometimes when things may be falling apart they may
actually be falling into place.*

Anonymous

'But you know, it can all change on a sixpence,' I told
my friend Lisa, whom I hadn't seen in a while, on Sunday,
November 22 2015. She and I were on a coach in Poland.
It was a weekend trip involving a flight to Kracow. On the
way, we were catching up with my life. Which looked rosy.
All my four children were happy and doing well; three
had left home because they'd grown up, one was still at
school, my husband Christian was in a good job at the top
of his career and I had just started back in the film world,
my earliest passion and where I had worked before having
children. We were all fit and healthy.

Lisa sighed, revealing a few of her own family worries.

That was when I said: 'But it's all so fragile, it might be going well now for me… but it can all change on a sixpence.'

And four days after I'd said that, for me it did.

August 2015 Abersoch, North Wales. Main Beach. Summer Holidays

Monday morning, with the dancing sparkles of sunshine on the sea reflecting a sky-blue heaven above, but with a chilly wind. Windproof jackets zipped up to our chins. Two brown dogs, our nine-year-old chocolate Labrador Baloo and Jane's cocker spaniel, energetically weaving in and out of the breaking frothy waves, their tails wagging fast. Jane, a friend, recommended a book to me. Unusually for me, when I arrived back from walking Baloo, I ordered it straight away.

For the first time I felt I had the gift of time to be able to read a book again after twenty-five hectic years. The book was called *Do No Harm* by Dr Henry Marsh. Jane had apologised in advance for some of the upsetting, sad parts of the book. I read it. I enjoyed his writing and the insight into a brain surgeon's world and dealing with people who had got brain tumours.

I put it down and thought, *what very unfortunate people*, the way you do when you feel so sorry for people whose fates you never think will happen to you.

Only it did.

I was enjoying my work back in the film world, where I had trained as a film editor with the BBC. I felt quite the lady about town. I bought a new little black dress (£49 from Mango). I made several trips to London. I'd arranged to meet Kitty, my twenty-two-year old daughter and take her to lunch at The Ivy restaurant in the Kings Road, as she had a job with McLaren Formula One, which meant she was away a great deal, travelling the world.

I'd been experiencing dizziness and loss of balance for about a week and I knew something wasn't right with me physically, but it was a rare chance for a special mother/daughter day and I didn't want to cancel. I also thought it was just an ear infection that could easily be put right with antibiotics.

When Kitty and I met at the entrance to Sloane Square tube on Wednesday 9 2015, her face dropped in a concern bordering on horror because I was wobbly and had to hold on to any support I could find to not fall over. She took my arm, even though we had never been very touchy. I couldn't walk without help. She held onto me all that afternoon.

When we got back to the flat, Kitty phoned my mother Susannah, though we call her Gogo, and explained her concerns. Gogo asked to be put onto me.

'Gillian,' my mum said firmly. (Hearing my name in full always meant my mother meant business), 'make an appointment with the doctor now.'

'Yes, I will,' I said meekly and did so.

'First appointment tomorrow,' said the receptionist, 'do you mind a trainee?'

'No,' and then without thinking, 'can he refer me up if necessary?'

It was the first time I admitted to myself that this could be complicated.

Christian had also noticed something was wrong, with my frequent falls and had asked me to make a doctor's appointment before my mum. I knew he was right but our lives are so busy and linear: we don't like anything to interrupt our plans, and I had so many exciting plans. Apart from the day with Kitty there was a party to go to that night. I drank champagne and willed whatever it was making me unbalanced to go away.

Unknown to everyone except me my right hand had seized up and I couldn't write. This had happened quite suddenly on November 27 whilst presenting a client with the film he had commissioned. I had to make notes of the amends. Suddenly my hand seized up. I was so embarrassed I hid my hand behind the computer. I had to remember the amends later. And I had two strange tremors. One went on for quite a few minutes. My right leg started convulsing uncontrollably. There was no pain but it scared me so much I denied the fits any credence: I put them down to muscle fatigue, or sitting in the car for too long. When I got out of the car I fell straight over as though completely drunk. I even laughed as it felt like that iconic scene in the film *Arthur* where Dudley Moore does just that in front of a police officer and calls the guy an 'ocifer'. But I was just pushing fear right back down where it was coming from.

I still hoped it would all just go away.

When my alarm woke me in London it was so early and I got up quickly, much too quickly and fell straight over. I picked myself up and wished Christian was coming with me home to Cheshire, by taxi, train and car to my doctor's appointment at eight thirty a.m.

Our two taxis arrived at five a.m. Christian's was taking him to Heathrow to fly to Germany on business, mine was dropping me off at Euston to catch the six a.m. train north for the appointment. I watched his taxi drive away to the airport and felt very lonely. I needed him beside me. But I didn't want to be needy and get in the way of my husband's working life. 'I'm fine, I can manage on my own,' is a mum's standard answer even though there are many times, especially when the children are small, that we long for help and really do need it. That day, in hindsight, was one of them.

It was a cold morning. I was wearing a warm coat, but on the platform at Euston, even after a hot cup of tea, I shivered uncontrollably waiting for the train. Even on the train I couldn't seem to get warm. At Crewe it was raining hard and I had quite a long walk to the car. I drove into the doctor's surgery car-park with relief that the journey was over. I actually thought I would be driving the car home about half an hour later.

I had a smart outfit ready to change into after the appointment. It was supposed to be my first day working for Richard Knew at Knew Productions and it was a networking lunch at the Grovesnor Hotel in Chester.

There in the waiting-room, I thought about a warm bed…
closing my eyes and sleep.

At about half past eight in the morning a polite young
newly-trained doctor asked what he could do for me.

'I think I have an ear infection,' I said.

He shone his torch into my ears and shook his head.

'There's no infection,' he said.

'Well, OK,' I said, finally and reluctantly facing the
truth, 'my right arm and right leg have gone weak.'

He quietly did a few pushing and pulling tests of my
arms and legs, he tapped my knees for reflexes and said
'Excuse me, I'm just going to refer this to a more senior
doctor.'

I was alarmed. I thought I had performed quite well in
the pushing and pulling exercises, had really done my best,
so not much could be wrong could it?

It had crossed my mind a few times that I might have
had a minor stroke.

My own doctor, a lady called Dr. Saggar, whom I knew
from previous visits with the children, entered and carried
out the same pushing and pulling and reflex tests on my
arms and legs.

'How did you get here?' she asked.

When I told her she put her arm over her face and said,
'No, no, you should never have driven here!'

I thought *it's definitely a stroke I've had*.

'But I'm fine now so can I drive home and just rest?'

Very gently she said, 'It's unlikely it's a stroke. I'm calling you an emergency ambulance to take you to Leighton Hospital. You need further tests.'

'Oh,' I said, 'so, I can't just quickly drive home first?

'No.' She shook her head. Rather too sadly I thought.

'Oh… so…'

My brain tried to catch up and compute this U-turn of the day. *So I still might make the business lunch, if they're quick at the hospital… no, they're never quick at any hospital and it looks like I have had a small stroke and they can't confirm it…* so as the business lunch began to fade I knew I would soon need to tell the production company that I was reneging on my first engagement, on my first day. That went very much against my work ethic. I put it off another half hour, still hoping that the doctors had overreacted and I was actually going to have a normal day again.

When the ambulance arrived and I climbed in I felt this was all an overreaction on the part of my kind lady doctor. I apologized to the paramedics. I felt a fraud and wished I could just go quietly home.

But they were kind and thorough and left me in a day ward. What now?

I had managed a quick call to Christian only to start crying as soon as I heard his voice. He was just coming in to land in Frankfurt.

'I think I've had a stroke,' I blubbed and then couldn't speak.

I was called through to a small room and a young doctor did the same pushing and pulling tests on my arms and legs.

Again I thought I had done rather well and thought maybe they would let me go home after all.

But he said, 'I think this needs further looking into.'

Hopes dashed.

I sat back in the chair in the day ward and waited.

A woman arrived with acute breathing problems and was put on oxygen.

Another woman in a nearby room was being violently sick. She had hardly any hair. *Chemotherapy*, I thought and felt desperatly sorry for her. Hospitals catch us when we fall, but we want to be back in the world, living our lives.

I realised I really wasn't going to make the lunch and texted Richard to say I was in hospital.

Margaret, his wife and colleague, texted back, *I hope it's nothing too serious.*

Time passed. I still hoped everyone was overreacting or being over-cautious.

Later that morning I was taken by wheelchair for a CT scan.

They were politely efficient as I was wheeled in and I was politely acquiescent. I had seen a CT scanner with my son a couple of years earlier. It was a machine that wouldn't have looked out of place in a *Star Wars* film.

They saw me politely into the scanner. When the scan was over two men came out of the room with all the screens. They and the nurses were all too nice. *The kinder the nurses get you know the worse it is*, I began to think. They all came out and gently lifted me up off the scan bed.

I suspected they had seen something that was not good. I decided to take each moment by moment. At least that's what I think my brain did; it was too much for it to jump ahead to unknown grim conclusions.

They wheeled me back to my chair in the day room where I watched the events of a day in hospital come, be resolved and go. I realised I had been there the longest and felt lonely. Even the nurses had changed shifts. Faces and characters, which had become familiar in a few hours, had gone and I felt left behind. I was offered lunch and tea and it helped pass the day. I also realised, with mixed feelings of trepidation and surprise, that I was relieved to just be sitting doing nothing, as I couldn't have coped with a business lunch.

I looked at my phone and saw texts from Kitty and from Phillipa, whom we all call Philly, Christian's number two in his business. Philly knows our family well and has seen all the children grow up. So I replied to them and we exchanged texts. I give the texts verbatim.

From Kitty: Hi! Not sure if you are able to get onto your phone! Dad has just told me! Are you ok??? I'm right here if you need me! Can get on a train at anytime! Please call if you can! Let me know! Ready on stand by to come!! You are in the best hands thank god you went to the doctor when you did!! Love you lots! Let me know if you are allowed to talk and I'll ring!! Xxxxxxxxx

Me to Kitty: Hi - just waiting for an X-Ray - sorry for the drama - glad we had our mum and daughter day!! I'll let you know results as soon as I do. Xx

Kitty: No not drama at all!! What hospital are you at? I'm waiting to come home I want to be there with you! If you are able to talk on the phone let me know and I'll ring you! Lots of love please be ok!! Xxxxx

Me to Kitty: I'm at Leighton. I'm waiting for a CT scan. Are you at work? I'll let you know as soon as I know anything. No don't worry - keep your plans to see Gogo and Grandpa - I'll let you know as soon as I do. Can't speak at the moment. Dad flying back tonight. Xxxx

Kitty: I'm coming to see you! Philly is driving me up now, I want to be there, you shouldn't be on your own xxx

Me to Kitty: Oh gosh - well that's really lovely. I am at Leighton - but you don't have transport and nor do I. I'm in Ward 2. What of it's nothing and you go to all this effort? I'll feel a fraud

Kitty: We'll figure something out! I want to be there with you Mum don't stress, I really hope it is nothing. xx

Me to Kitty: I'm going for a CT scan at 2.30 so won't be in the ward. Where are you? Are you on the train or is Philly driving? Xx

Kitty: Philly's driving me all the way up to you

Me: Oh I can't believe it! Honestly - you're both amazing. I am feeling OK- just want to know what it is. See you soon. –xx

Kitty: It's our pleasure! Just want you to be ok! And trust me we are both praying that it's an ear infection or something small like that!! Lots of love xxx

Me: Bless you both! Ear infection has been ruled out! Xx

I heard a young English nurse flirting with a Spanish doctor. She was quite forward and he handled it very well, remaining friendly but professional. At about four o'clock in the afternoon the Spanish doctor, who was the general ward consultant, came to my little cubicle, where I was still sitting on a chair.

He was holding a file of papers. He had come to tell me what the scan had revealed.

The tiny part of me, which said he was going to say it was nothing and I could go home, faded when I saw his face. His kind, intelligent eyes trying to be neutral and yet I detected sorrow in them.

'Would you like to come with me?' he said.

Do I have to, I thought…?

I stood up. I felt heavy adrenalin swirling in the pit of my stomach.

He turned and then turned back to me, 'Have you got anyone here with you? Any family?'

'My daughter is arriving soon,' I said, as though trying to reassure him.

'Would you rather wait till she is here?'

So this is serious now and the seconds seemed to slow down.

'No,' I said firmly. 'Tell me now.'

We walked down the sterile corridor. The executioner's kind assistant and me. He stopped outside his private office and asked again, advising, 'Are you sure you wouldn't rather wait for your family to be with you? It may be better if they were with you.'

I knew then and yet I didn't. I still had no inkling of what it was except that it was serious. Oh! For heaven's sake, tell me now. Right now. Let's get this waiting hell over with.

'No,' I said politely, 'please tell me.'

We went into his room and he asked me to sit down.

I sat down. So did he.

He looked me straight in the eyes and said…

(Even now I expected a stay of execution).

He spoke slowly and clearly.

'You have a brain tumour.'

I got as far as the word 'tumour' and his mouth went into slow motion. I even thought what a perfect shape his lips made as he said the word 'tumour' with his beautifully accented English. I realised this was the consultant the nurse had been flirting with earlier and how well he had handled it and why she had been flirting with him.

The brain will do anything to scamper out of having to focus on the shock ignited right in front of it. Normal life fights hard to keep a hold and carry on in its expected and linear fashion. It was easier musing on him and all the coloured medical diagrams on the wall behind his head than on listening to what he was actually telling me. Which I didn't want to hear.

'Oh,' I said absently, 'a tumour?'

'Yes.' He spoke it firmly and clearly and searched my eyes to see how much my brain had scampered away and back, away and back, like an over-excited springer spaniel before a walk.

'In my brain?'

'Yes'. He nodded, evidently relieved I seemed to have understood.

'How big is it?' I asked.

26

He looked at the notes and formed a circle with his thumb and forefinger around the size of a two-penny piece.

I had no idea if that was good news or bad so I asked, 'is it operable?'

Do No Harm flashed into my brain. I thought I had morphed into Dr. Henry Marsh's book like the children did into Narnia. Only that was an exciting adventure land from my childhood. Magical. This was not.

'I think so,' he replied. 'But I can't give you a definite answer to that question.'

The 'I think so' lodged as an affirmative to me. One tiny piece of flotsam to cling to in a sea of death.

'So is it… is it cancer?'

'Yes. It is.'

I nodded. They know not to say too much at this point. I must have seemed calm.

'Well,' I said and looked at him and smiled, 'thank goodness it's me.'

He looked confused.

'Me and not one of the children,' I added quietly.

Two years earlier, Robin, my youngest son, aged twelve at the time, had developed a severe pain in his shinbone. Initially I thought it was growing pains but then googled and found that a pain in one leg should be checked out. We went to the doctor and she sent him for an X-ray. I received the message that it had come back clear.

He spent the next nine months coping with severe pain in his leg hiding it at school and I emptied the chemists of Calpol.

We went to five doctors who all said, 'Was the X-ray clear?' or words to that effect, to which I replied, 'Yes, it came back clear.' And then they would just dismiss us.

Eventually the pain was too insistent and had clearly gone on for too long.

I made a doctor's appointment and (not for the first time in my life in a busy doctor's surgery) said I wasn't leaving until something was done for my poor child. Blood tests followed and we had been referred to an orthopaedic children's oncology ward, where the consultant took less than a minute to see they had X-rayed the wrong part of his leg. The correct part was X-rayed and there was the dark circle of a tumour as clear as anything.

Robin was lying down behind me. The consultant and I were looking at the tumour on the X-ray. I was very close to his jacket lapels and my hands reached out towards him as if to grab them and beg him to give me the tumour. Not this little boy with his life ahead of him. I had to wait for two days for the results of scans and accurate diagnosis. It was benign, operated and removed.

Sorrow wandered past the door but he didn't come knocking that time. But I saw him and his frightening shadowy presence.

I knew I would have taken that tumour from Robin. I didn't need to, it was operated on and it was non-malignant and has not returned.

Hence, my own reaction to my diagnosis, that so surprised the Spanish consultant giving me the news.

The Spanish consultant was saying some other things but they were muddled as my swollen brain and weak body sought to protect me from the appalling news. The spinning room, his muffled voice and everything in slow motion and then he was ushering me out and he left me on my own rather quickly to make a phone call.

I wandered back to my hard plastic utilitarian chair in the ward, unsure of where to go and what to do. I even wondered fleetingly whether if I walked out at that moment, perhaps no one would notice and all this horror would go away.

I wanted to close the curtains around the chair but I couldn't seem to pull them tight, ineffectual things that they are. No one knew what I had just been told and the nurses were busy dealing with all the myriad of things they have to do and no one came to help me.

Pathetic thing they probably thought, when I asked one of them to pull the flimsy curtain across for me and with irritation she did because I must have just looked lazy.

As soon as I had the dim light of the closed curtains around me and I was on my own, the words 'brain tumour' finally somehow clarified inside me.

I had a cousin and two friends who had had brain tumours and they all had died within months. I began to cry tears of realisation, that my life was not just entering its graceful autumnal era, but had leapt forward to the end of its winter. I felt totally abandoned and wished so much for Kitty to arrive.

How far away are you? I texted.

I had never needed someone, family, before like this and I ached for her to arrive.

Another wait on my own.

I sat very still. I was nervous of having to tell her: to burst her happy disposition and the excitement of exploring her young life with this news.

I did wonder why the consultant would tell me such news but not tell the nurses too. He had seemed distracted at the end.

I found out later when a Spanish nurse arrived in a hurry and told me to immediately take several pills. Her English was not good enough to explain what they were, which she felt embarrassed by. She was very smiley and sweet.

Apparently the CT scan had showed such a large swelling in the brain around the tumour, hence the reason for my symptoms, that the priority was to get a high dose of steroids down me as quickly as possible. He thought I had taken the news remarkably well, so he got on with the business of ordering the emergency medication. It's a large hospital and getting medication can take a long time. I was left with the feeling that he thought my head was about to explode.

Suddenly my daughter Kitty put her pretty head with her glossy brown hair around the curtain and with her uplifting smile said, 'Mum!' as though she had come across me by chance.

Emotions took over and I collapsed into her warm embrace and very fluffy purple hood and cried into her neck, 'Oh Kitty, I've got a brain tumour!'

It was such a relief telling someone. But it didn't make the tumour go away and at that moment I knew that however long I had, I would never be released of this sentence. Parole maybe, but never freedom.

I saw Philly's face crumple with sorrow and shock. She was standing beside the curtain giving Kitty and me time to hold each other.

She disappeared. Months later I found out that she went and fought for me to be able to go home that night.

They wanted to keep me in hospital. Philly also went and brought the car nearer and got us a free pass out of the car park. What an organiser! It was about six o'clock in the evening. 'Make sure you're back by seven in the morning,' the nurse whispered kindly, conspiratorially but sternly.

Time has its own rules in hospitals. Emerging out of the hospital, I felt I had entered a different world, darker and bleaker than the one I had left that morning.

It was very dark, no moon and the car park was indeed bleak and I walked out of hospital an altered person, never again to be entirely the Gilly I'd been. The swing-gate opened automatically for us. A small act of kindness by a nurse who knew the news I had just been given. These small acts of kindness, ever since that first one, have been the little rays of sunlight that have make living with a brain tumour bearable.

Kitty texted Cal, my eldest son, who was on standby to get on a train and get home.

You need to come home. Just get on the train, she texted. She didn't want to tell him the news.

Jens, my third child, was in America on a placement year abroad as part of his university course. Christian had asked Kate, a friend, to take Robin home from school with her, which she did without question: you need friends like that.

I longed for all my family home with me to absorb this news and at the same time I was frightened of telling them, partly because I just wanted to have a normal evening. Philly drove Kitty and me to collect Robin, she had already driven over two hundred and fifty miles bringing Kitty to me. Kitty went in.

'Is Mum OK?' he asked immediately in our friend Kate's house. Kitty didn't want to tell him the truth there and then.

'Yes,' said Kitty.

But as soon as he climbed in I told him straightaway. The darkness inside the car helped.

He took the news silently. He was fourteen.

As Philly was driving us back home, Christian rang. I didn't want to answer because I didn't want to tell him over the phone.

'You have to answer,' said Philly beside me, 'he's worried sick.'

I answered the phone. 'I'm so sorry,' I told my husband. 'Darling, I've got a brain tumour.'

Sorry for our future that looked like it had been stolen from us. Sorry for being stupid enough to even get a brain tumour. Sorry for Christian, sorry for the kids and I allowed some self-pity.

I also rang my mum and told her.

Christian had the terrible job of ringing Jens in the USA, carefree in sunny Miami, enjoying a placement year away.

This was how Jens felt when Christian told him.

The hardest thing I've ever had to do was to hang up the phone, not knowing when I would next speak to Mum again. I was alone. And my world turned upside down in a matter of minutes.

I regretted not trying to say more, but the words I thought of, I couldn't physically say. I only really remember the static silence over the phone after receiving the news that mum had been diagnosed with a brain tumour. At first I was very confused, not being able to see her made it very difficult for me to come to grips with her awful news. I just wanted to hug her. I never expected something like this to happen to us. But as the news sunk in, not knowing how long Mum had to live, I couldn't help but think of every outcome. Thinking of a world without my mum in it haunted me. I felt helpless, guilty and was oblivious to everything and everyone around me. Everything that seemed important to me before now was insignificant. And all my problems except this seemed to be all of a sudden very solvable. But most of all I was scared, not really knowing what I was returning to. For me it was impossible to imagine the mum I knew to be in a weaker form. All that mattered to me was to get home.

Meanwhile we had arrived home to be greeted warmly by Baloo, our chocolate Labrador.

Good God! I thought in surprise as I walked in the door, 'I won't even have to mourn the dog!' Baloo welcomed us home, in the moment. He was only nine: I would die before him! Yet he was unaware that his life would be affected too.

Christian had received my first tearful call at nine that morning. He had taken his employee to the office, introduced her to the relevant bosses and left straight away to catch the next flight home to Manchester. He was supposed to be staying in Germany for two days.

When he arrived home he wrapped me in the strongest hug and he let out a deep guttural howl of anguish. The children watched us and I think that was the first time they saw the depth of our love. At different points Robin suddenly cried and came and hugged me, Cal hugged me and Kitty had in the hospital. We are not a huggy family. We learned quickly. Everything had changed.

That Thursday, December 10, was a surreal evening. Seemingly normal. The five of us, Jens missing, eating supper. I couldn't eat. Cal slept on the sofa downstairs with the bright Christmas tree and fairy lights shining over the fireplace. Light to keep the darkness at bay. I joined him at some point in the night. Comfort in togetherness.

2
THE WAITING GAME

Autumnal - nothing to do with leaves. It is to do with
a certain brownness at the edges of the day... Brown is
creeping up on us, take my word for it... Russets and
tangerine shades of old gold flushing the very outside
edge of the senses... deep shining ochre's, burnt umber
and parchments of baked earth - reflecting on itself and
through itself, filtering the light. At such times, perhaps,
coincidentally, the leaves might fall, somewhere, by
repute. Yesterday was blue, like smoke.

Rosencrantz and Guildenstern are Dead
(1966) Tom Stoppard

I was back in the ward by seven in the morning. Hard plastic chairs again.

Today was a day of further tests to see if it was a primary or secondary tumour.

Lots of waiting. But all the nurses were kind and good. They all knew now.

First I had a mammogram – they immediately told me it was all clear.

Later I had an MRI scan, during which I listened to a Rachmaninov concerto – almost the whole composition as MRIs take quite a long time. I also had a needle, to inject a contrast dye into my blood for a better view of the tumour.

The first of so many needles.

For the MRI scan I had to remove all my clothes and then put on a hospital gown. But I was allowed to keep my socks on. They had been sent to me as a present from America by one of my oldest, closest friends, Caroline Socha, and when sending them she could never have realised the significance of what they would become to me. It felt as though there was a part of her there, she was there, close to me, holding my feet, wrapping them in warmth and care. I make sure I always wear socks from someone special for all my MRIs. My mother's and younger sister's also feel good. Never underestimate the importance and strength a friend's socks can give you! Caroline's was with me in all my scans, Mum's on the day of the operation, Cecelia's to help me through the routine blood tests. Toes cosily wrapped up in friendship and love from someone else.

I went for a CT scan that searched for secondary tumours.

When I was waiting with just the porter and a nurse in the corridor, she must have felt the need to fill the silence. So she told me about this woman who had gone for a CT scan thinking nothing was wrong and came out only to be told the cancer now was all over her body and three weeks later she was dead!

'Oh, poor lady,' I said politely, mustering the strength not to say, *are you too insensitive to appreciate what you've just said? Don't you know that I may be in the same position?*

The hospital porter was stunned. I could feel his shock coming in waves behind my head. They're always so sensitive. It takes a very special person to be a hospital porter. Kind, tactful, not too interfering, and a good trolley driver.

He blurted out with embarrassment; 'I've just booked my holiday to Tenerife!' This was hardly appropriate but presumably all he could think of, given the circumstances.

Later, when Christian was allowed to rejoin us the porter recovered his normal sense of banter.

'Who's this fellow who keeps following you behind the trolley?' he asked.

'I've no idea!' I replied.

Christian replied in Baloo's gruff voice, 'Oh, I'm just the faithful Labrador, Christian.'

He's always been good at voices and sounds.

He made me laugh. I imagined Baloo and him tramping along behind the trolley together.

Wit, in times of stress, can be the release of a pressure valve.

A friend, who does hypnotherapy work with cancer patients, happened to be in the hospital that day and came and saw us. It seemed strange to see him in his professional role when I had only ever seen him socially. I would be seeing him a lot more in his professional role.

And then we waited. The children arrived and played a game of cards.

Everything felt displaced. There were the children playing cards, a game they played thousands of times on holiday, but here they were playing it in the stark surroundings of the day ward as a distraction.

It was a long day.

At five p.m. the same Spanish consultant walked in.

We had decided we should all hear the news together.

'No,' he said, 'just you and your husband.'

I think that was one of the worst moments.

The children looked ashen. My legs felt heavy. I was walking in to a summary execution with no hope of appeal for clemency from whatever or whoever had polluted my body with this tumour. Christian looked suddenly older. I looked at him and I realised in my subconscious that he'd always assumed he would die before me and I thought that too. There was more longevity in my family than his. Not so now.

I thought about that lady who had secondary tumours all over her body. Would I be the same? Would I even see Christmas? But his news was good. No secondary tumours. Just a primary brain tumour!

In the world of tumours, that's comparatively good news.

Cal, Kitty and Robin wrote how they felt when the consultant asked for just Christian and I to go in and hear the news.

Cal:

When the consultant asked to see Mum and Dad privately we felt it wasn't good news, we expected the worst. Kitty, Robin and I were left alone in the ward to wait. We did not talk, we simply sat, stood, and paced as each of us contemplated what the result might be and what impact it would have on mum's life and our own.

It was fifteen minutes, I am told, before they came out to deliver the news. My memory is those fifteen minutes felt more like two hours. It was without question the hardest and longest fifteen minutes I have endured in my life to date.

I remember the impossible task of trying to answer questions that could not be answered. In this moment all I knew was that Mum had a brain tumour, diagnosed the day before. A brain tumour was something that sounded so serious and scary you felt it was the end almost immediately. I sat in a chair next to the hospital bed and played through in my head endless different scenarios that in turn had a multitude of different possibilities and outcomes. Each second that went by would produce another question – has the tumour spread? Would Mum live to see Christmas? Spring? What will happen to Dad? To us? These were questions that could not be answered in that moment so I was left answering them by assuming the worst, which would subsequently produce another question. And so it was a vicious circle that slowly took me deeper and darker into a parallel life that wasn't my own, but one that I was slowly realising was becoming a reality.

The longer the wait continued the deeper and darker I went, it became almost unbearable, like your own life is slowly being taken away from you. Bizarrely it began to feel like I had the tumour, like I was carrying it and that my own life had suddenly been cut short.

All three of us remained silent throughout, all knowing we were asking the same questions, but knowing we could not speak for fear someone would be in an even darker place, or that you yourself would take them to one. We all kept looking down the corridor longing for the consultant's door to open and put an end to the wait.

I haven't yet been back to the depths of that dark place in the ups and downs in the time since the diagnosis. I think it was the fear of not knowing that made those fifteen minutes so difficult. We know our battle now and whilst the beast sometimes changes, we know what we are fighting. We know it is a long and hard battle and one we are eventually likely to lose. But that doesn't stop our hope.

Kitty:

The feeling of your world crashing down, the most terrible news you could hear in your lifetime, there isn't really anything to prepare you for it. There's no slow dramatic music on top of a movie montage blasting through life as you know it, no hunky doctor rushing in ready to save the day, just a cold large shared hospital room and a little Spanish doctor coming over to say 'no I think it's best the kids don't hear what I have to say'.

Fifteen minutes. Fifteen whole minutes of the unknown. As a family we are well known for brushing over serious situations with black humour and jokes, but there was nothing to say during the time it took the doctor to tell my parents that mum had a terminal brain tumour. You can imagine his surprise when we celebrated this fact fifteen minutes later. We were fearing the worst, we thought they'd come back and say she was riddled with cancer and had a mere three weeks left, so when our fifteen minutes was up and we saw mum and dad smiling their way down the ward we were thrilled, it was the best news. 'Mum only has a brain tumour? That's fantastic!'

We did get our movie moment as we were leaving the hospital, we all stopped, just like that, no words, we just huddled as a family and hugging and praying that we can beat this. We were crying, the nurses were crying, we were just short of a George Clooney lookalike running down the ward, from an episode of ER.

It's something no one can prepare you for, something you imagine from time to time but never think you'll be the person it happens to: that your family will be chosen with this tragedy.

We aren't the religious type, but each of us were praying in those fifteen minutes, wishing for a something to bring us good news, and in a way our prayers were answered, mum is still here fighting each day and our family is still praying to beat it together

Robin:

Leaning nervously against the wall I studied the consultant as he walked into the ward to deliver news that would change the fate of all our lives. When the consultant stated that he wanted to chat with mum and Dad in private my siblings and I were left to the abyss of our minds that were already assuming the worst outcome. The ward was filled with the noises of ill-looking patients accompanied by the chatter and frantic rushing of the nurses, yet in-spite of this organised chaos I had never felt more alone. As a fourteen year old kid you never even question the possibility that your mum could be taken away from you yet here I was looking out the hospital window thinking about that very scenario.

I was powerless and in this moment all I could do was pray. Never before had I been religious yet at that time it was the only slice of hope that was left. Praying, I hoped for there to be no more cancer, I hoped for things to selfishly turn to normal ultimately I prayed for this whole thing to be over so I could get back to the average teenagers life. My siblings were in the same state and we only exchanged the odd eye contact. After *what seemed like an eternity I turned to the clock to see only five minutes had passed. I watched every person who passed the ward to see if they were the consultant or just someone who could end this on going mind game. Finally fifteen minutes had passed on the clocks and we were met by Dad, who had a smile like a slice of hope, upon which we followed him to the consultant's office to hear the full story.*

When I gathered up my belongings of that long day, a nurse who had been there all day said to me, 'You'll be fine. You'll be fine.'

I looked hard into her eyes. How did she know? I wanted to say that but I didn't.

I wanted to believe her.

In the reception area, just before leaving, the five of us grouped close together and hugged, we were getting good at this hugging thing! Not just a superficial hug but a really tight and long hug. The nurse at the reception desk started crying.

So began the days of adjusting to living with dying: or dying with living.

But as someone pointed out to me one day soon after: 'We're all of us dying.'

The days that followed were all a strange mix of normal life with all its minutiae and waiting for an appointment to meet my neurologist.

My mother and youngest sister, Cecelia, came to stay and offer support and help.

I had had a 'complex' relationship with my younger sister. For years at times we did not really speak, because we never aired minor misunderstandings which then became major misunderstandings. And I always went to my older sisters for confidences. Sometimes it was really bad and I felt huge animosity from her towards me and I struggled to understand her apparent dislike of me. But I know it takes two, so I simply came to the conclusion she just didn't like me. We tried to get the cousins together from time to time but there were so many lost opportunities. The whole thing upset me hugely.

My two personal demons are a) rejection and b) fearing no one likes me, so I pretty quickly realised I couldn't be an actress, something I yearned to be since my mum took me to see *Mary Poppins* when I was three and I longed to be part of the magical world of film, stage and story-telling.

Actually it had got to such a stalemate of not communicating with my younger sister that it never occurred to me she would even care or be interested in my illness. How wrong could I have been? Cecelia had immediately booked her flight from Jersey, where she lives, and driven my mother up to Cheshire.

Of all the things that have come out of my tumour, the immediate love and unconditional support and deep rapprochement we have gone through since has been one of the most wonderful and deeply enlightening. I went to bed the night they arrived with a deep sense of real contentment; of renewal, regrets for wasted time but at least we had time to make up and the warmest times they have been.

How ironic that I was happier that night than I had been in all the years of our life together. Cecelia has looked after me many times since that first visit, including one very frightening epileptic fit, which she had read up about what to do and handled brilliantly. I always look forward to her visits. Cecelia and I have spoken once of the silly sibling rivalry that caused it; and I saw it from her side, as she saw it from mine, but we've put it all behind us and will just make the most of the time we do have now being close. I'm so grateful for the time we've had to make up and the warmth that brings. It felt healing and has done so ever since like the steady soft constant warmth a candle brings.

My family, parents and three sisters immediately became connected daily and very close. Having been separated over thousands of miles for most of our lives, in places hard to communicate with, in Africa, it felt good to be so together and so in touch again. My parents had planned and we had been to 'get togethers' either in Africa or the UK and they had been fun. My mother announced very strongly at one of them the paramount importance of family. But we had never had that day-to-day stuff of life-sharing, that families have who live close by each other. Everything had to be planned well in advance and involved expensive flights. A consequence of our peripatetic childhood. My father worked for Shell and this took him on postings to various parts of the world.

Jacky sent this Whatsapp:

Hi Gilly. I have been awake since 4am! There is most definitely a greater being or force out there guiding us along a

path of our own destiny. Never before have we all felt so close,
and so strongly.

I had a post-shock panic attack early one morning in the week following my diagnosis and we called the ambulance. I felt a fraud, 'Oh, you are no faker!' they replied kindly. We listened to Michael Buble singing soothing Christmas songs all the way to the hospital.

A and E was quiet. The consultant was a kind and caring Syrian. A and E at what was left of any hospital in his whole country would have been a horror scene, everywhere and almost everyone was getting bombed to bits. I really did feel a faker.

Meeting my neurosurgeon
I was so glad now I had read Henry Marsh's book, although people subsequently advised against it if they didn't know I had. I had read it as soon as Jane recommended it to me the previous summer and also given it to my mother to read. It gave me an insight into how the person who I was about to meet would be seeing the situation. Not faceless, not cynical, just trying to make the best medical decision for someone's life sitting in front of them.

Waiting to meet my neurosurgeon felt like waiting to see the headmaster when you knew you'd been in trouble. I had asked Christian to put a jacket on. Silly really – as though it matters when he has to make a medical evidence-based decision. But I was doing anything to get him on my side.

I have been lucky always to have good health, never smoked, not overweight, love sport and exercise... a good diet... so why?

Eventually after waiting in a side-room we were called in.

I immediately liked the look of him. His name was Rupert Price. He had a kind face and intelligent eyes. He had just come out of theatre and was wearing a cartoon surgical hat.

The first thing he asked me was did I have any children?

'Yes,' I allowed myself deep pride, 'four.'

'Tell me about them,' he said, gently.

I started with Cal and then said I had a daughter called Kitty.

'I've a daughter called Kitty too,' he said.

It was as though an almost palpable benign force suddenly entered the space between us. Everything was going to be all right. We had daughters the same age and the same unusual name and I knew that we were going to get along. It's important to like the person who is going to open your head up and delve inside. After mentioning the other two which was simply giving him time to think he said, 'would you like me to do your operation?'

I did not hesitate, I didn't want anyone else. Not with Kittys in common!

He sprang into action. Today was the eighteenth of December, just one week before Christmas Day. He was going try and work magic and squeeze me in before Christmas, before everything closed down for that two-week festive period. I was desperate to have the operation quickly and didn't want to wait three more weeks with the

46

tumour aggressively growing inside me. It felt like a hostile alien that would burst out of my head when we were eating Christmas lunch like the iconic scene with John Hurt from the film *Alien*.

Then came the chat about the type of tumour he thought I had. Pretty bad. He said it was usually a year to fourteen months prognosis. But he had one patient who had reached five years.

We took this news silently.

He delivered it very well. Kindly, but without hiding any facts and never, ever, patronising.

We were whisked downstairs for me to have one of many blood tests to get ready for the operation on the following Monday. Rupert had definitely pulled out all the stops.

A pretty young nurse of Caribbean origin called Consuela did one of the tests pre-admission tests. She exuded peace and calm. As she took my details she said,

'You'll be fine, all is well with your soul.'

I emerged from that test to find Christian had gone into shock. Literally, white and not quite with it. The next nurse also quickly noticed and we both had to look after him, offer 'Tea and Sympathy' as the Carole King song goes. Ironic: I'm the one with the tumour, I pointed out to him. But it was a realisation of how much I meant to him. Only revealing itself in heightened times of tragedy the strength of his love for me was beginning to manifest itself, which we don't often take the time to acknowledge in our busy lives.

That night was Robin's school Christmas Carol concert in Chester Cathedral. I had never missed one. I wanted to go but be invisible: not ready to face anyone yet. So we crept in late, in the dark.

The vast and yet tranquil space of worship was filled with candles, fiercely glowing as though locked in a flickering war against the darkness all around threatening to engulf them. And then as if to help them solo voices soaring, joined by others. Powerful stuff: darkness and light. I didn't dutifully stand to sing, I half lay leaning on Christian, just loving the whole service. And I am not particularly religious: It's all just so familiar and what I have been brought up with. Normality. And normal was what I craved in my tumbling world. Any light I could grasp on my way down to smooth the bumps of such a sudden and dramatic fall.

I felt a great achievement and peace. Jane, my dog-walking, book-recommending friend from the beach came up and said nothing but gave me the gentlest, longest warm wrap around hug. No words. Perfect. Her husband Steve said, 'I've always believed women are emotionally stronger than men.' So I will deal with it better than Christian! I thought back to the day at the hospital and agreed! Although, in truth, it is equally hard for the partner and many times Christian has said to me he wishes he could take it for me. Like I wanted to for Robin. The strength of love.

A couple of weeks earlier it had been Robin's parents' evening. Dashing around all the teachers, he had walked several corridors ahead of me, so I was not close to him in front of his mates. The embarrassment of me! Normal for teenage boys. As we left the cathedral that evening he put his arm over my shoulder and walked hugging me close to him, in front of all his friends' curious stares. I felt so honoured. Almost worth getting a tumour. Well, perhaps that's going too far.

During that week of waiting I got into the habit of going silently downstairs between one and two o'clock in the silent hours of the morning, and making hot tea and a bowl of porridge with some honey from Kirsty's bees in the North Welsh hills. We had made a film together about her bees, so every spoonful had good healing memories.

I would light a candle that had been given to me by friends, trying their best to give me some light in my darkest hours.

At first Baloo got extremely excited at this new pattern of early waking. He would jump up excitedly wagging his tail and head straight for the door for breakfast! Gradually it became just a lift of the head, then just a sleepy thump of the tail, and then just one eye briefly opened.

I decided it was fine to pamper myself, so I wear some special knickers, and use soaps, candles, and little luxuries I had been saving for a rainy day. Now it was thunderous.

I enjoyed every moment, slowly, not rushing, because I couldn't. I took care over tiny things. I enjoyed natural things like the newest buds peeping through, it was an unusually warm December. I became quite good at predicting the first tweet of the early morning birds.

Having a long bath at school run time, not clock watching, not driving. No stress.

Brand new pillowcase and duvet cover!

All scented smells, natural and perfumed bath oils were brought into sharp focus and heightened.

My friends can't complain about having a head cold.

Christian and I were even more loving than usual. We became so close to each other.

And I felt lucky.

Still me: 'same same.... but different' as the T-shirt slogan from South East Asia says. We had brought a couple back for Robin and Jens.

I have been given a golden ticket to enjoy myself for as long as I have left.

I wanted to spend some time at home. Older age, disguised as frailty, had entered uninvited: she had come to stay. After racing through life at a hectic speed, taking every opportunity, working hard and having fun and almost always being healthy, it's liberating not worrying about ageing. Don't you dare erase the story of my life on my face! Each wrinkle and line on my face is a part of my story, my life. In our 'youth and beauty' culture I had felt guilty growing old.

I had thought about applying back to the BBC who had spent time and money giving me a training of excellence. But I felt when they saw my age on the application form they would roll around the floor laughing at me because, even though I didn't want to be on screen, through the visual medium of television, we live in a culture where we have made youth and beauty everything.

Of course there were downsides too. So often I would think, why has this happened to me?

If I ever allowed myself to feel melancholy, I found myself singing 'Something Good', that song from *The Sound of Music*, only I would change the last word. 'And somewhere in my youth or childhood, I must have done something… bad.'

The door going or the phone ringing, hearing a voice I don't know talking: equals stress. We soon didn't answer the landline. It took too much energy and performance.

Even people I did know coming around meant I had to put on a performance. They would walk cautiously in, in the early days, particularly after I had had surgery, not knowing if I may be or look completely different. I would reassure them I was still me! But that would take effort and it still does.

In my operation please mend my reversing fault. I have wiped out three cars in our own driveway. Of course this wish is ironic: I will never be allowed to drive again anyway.

I didn't realise how much I hated driving. But at least I had the choice – the women in Saudi didn't have that choice.

I've always loved buses and trains.

Please cut out jealousy, envy, greed, impatience, and prejudice.

Leave me patience, kindness and love.

Jens arrived home from sunny Miami where he was on a university year placement cruelly broken into by my diagnosis.

He was the picture of good health, tanned and still in bright, loose summer clothing. We had a very special homecoming lunch for him all six of us, together, for the first time in months. It almost hid what was coming: we had to leave at three p.m. to check into my neurological ward at four p.m. The briefest, but happiest, of snatched time, together.

Sunday December 20 2015- About four o'clock in the afternoon

As we drove down the drive to go to hospital I gave the family two strict instructions. 'Don't forget to pick up the turkey I've ordered' and 'please don't forget to put the bins out'. Which one do you think they remembered?

During the journey to the hospital to have brain surgery in the fast falling dusk of that grey, damp day, everything around me was vividly heightened. As though the colours and shapes of that winter afternoon in late December was an *Alice in Wonderland* tumble into a whole new surreal world. In many ways it has been.

3
INTO HOSPITAL

All the world is made of faith, and trust,
and pixie dust.

Peter Pan J.M. Barrie.

People have often asked me how I was feeling on that Sunday afternoon as I walked into my first neurological ward at North Staffordshire University Hospital for major brain surgery.

I knew that the operation was going to get rid of all the tumour they could reach. But I also saw that there's always someone worse off.

The first thing we all saw was a young boy, lying in bed with lots of tubes attached, very still, with his parents keeping watch in silent vigil over him. No child should ever have to go through this, I thought.

As Johnny Depp says as he goes around the wards playing Jack Sparrow from *Pirates of the Caribbean* at Great Ormond Street Hospital for children, 'it's the parents who are dying.'

I looked at the bleak-trying-to-be-OK-but-what-is-this-place-we-have-been-jettisoned-into faces of my children sitting in my hospital room. They needed something to do. Jens was there physically in his brightly coloured summer shorts. His mind was still wandering out of the warm waters of sun-soaked Miami Beach. Not snow-splashed Stoke on Trent.

I had hardly done any Christmas shopping and I wanted Christmas to be as normal for the children as possible.

Cal was promoted to chief Santa and with his three elves the four children went and did all the Christmas shopping in a very grey, cold and rainy Stoke-on-Trent, while I lay in my hospital bed.

When they arrived back at the ward they all looked ashen, grey and exhausted, as though they were the ones who needed brain surgery.

I sent them off to go and see the latest new *Star Wars* film and enter a more pleasant fantasy world.

Time for me to lie there and think

What is this life if full of care
We have no time to stop and stare.
No time to stand beneath the boughs
And stare as long as sheep and cows
No time to see, when woods we pass
Where squirrels hide their nuts in grass.
No time to see, in broad daylight,
Streams full of stars, like skies at night.
No time to turn at beauty's glance,
And watch her feet, how they can dance.
No time to wait till her mouth can
Enrich that smile her eyes began.
A poor life this, if full of care,
We have no time to stop and stare.

William Henry Davies
A poem my mother framed on the wall in the downstairs
loo of her home.

All the advertisements on the TV were insistently telling
me to 'Hurry, Hurry, Hurry!' Last chance. Offer must
end. It felt very peaceful knowing I didn't have to 'hurry,
hurry, hurry' in the pursuit to worship the new gods of
consumerism to keep their insatiable demands appeased.

However, I have always loved Christmas, a sign of a
happy childhood. And all those fairy lights at the darkest
time of year are a lift for the spirits. Cecelia worked in a
department store and would send lots of WhatsApp videos
and pictures of sparkling dresses and the festive scenes,
which was perfect. I loved virtual reality browsing around
her store and also felt part of her life and the outside world.
But I was glad not to have to 'Hurry, Hurry, Hurry!'

When two souls collide: Christian and I
The first time I met Christian he was upside down in
the air and crash-landing into the snow. He whooped with
laughter. *He looks like a fun person*, I thought.

It was December 1983, in a French resort called
Chamrousse, and we were both, separately then, on a
training course, to teach blind and disabled people to ski.
A friend had asked if I wanted to accompany her and on
the spur of the moment I had said yes. She asked if I would
like to get travel insurance, 'because you never know what
might happen!'

We trainers were to practise on each other before being
let loose on the disabled and blind skiers who had gamely

come along to be our guinea pigs. Christian and I were in the same small group and paired up: the fun guy I thought! He had to put on a blindfold and I had to guide him the safest route down the mountain calling instructions from behind: 'Left, right, right a bit more, left!'

Only I got my lefts and rights muddled up and sent him into all sorts of obstacles. He laughed at my panic, he was a funny sight and I was also laughing at the noises he was making as he fell. 'Sorry! I meant you to turn right!' as he hit another bump and fell over. He took off his blindfold and decided, he told me later, that this was the girl he was going to marry. Little Miss Earmuffs. He'd already checked me out on the coach from London and decided I looked too young! Wearing ridiculous earmuffs I probably did!

That evening we had to do some group work. Christian wooed me with his 'sound effects' and by the end of the evening I knew that this was the man I wanted to marry.

We would never have met if we hadn't gone on that course. We had no friends in common, our social circles didn't cross. It was pure chance, the collision of two souls finding each other and deciding instantly to spend the rest of their lives together.

We danced on that the sunny afternoon of our wedding day and have been dancing ever since (give or take a few arguments and the stuff of marriage!)

The Bicycle Ride: Victoria Station to Victoria Falls

In 1988 and 1989 just the two of us - Christian and I - undertook a one-year 10,000-mile bicycle ride down through Europe, Turkey, and into the African continent at Alexandria. Then through Sudan, Kenya, around

Lake Tanganyika, then south through Tanzania, Malawi, Zambia and Zimbabwe and to Victoria Falls. That's all another story but its relevance here is that it has informed all we do and our perspectives on life. Remembering what is really important: water, food, shelter, safety and the kindness and generosity of strangers.

I identified with the women, in that, after the above list, washing clothes became my chief concern. We only had a few and water in Africa is sometimes miles away. So whenever I saw a group of women washing their clothes, especially in Sudan, I would ask if I could wash my clothes too. The women would love a machine to do it for them, but we would sit and wash our clothes together and I would find huge comfort in their unity, their chat and their humour, which was sometimes gentle and sometimes surprisingly raucous. I had noticed the same in India too.

The camaraderie of laundry. I looked up once and saw a freshwater dolphin in Varanasi, a rare sight: its long beak and cheerful smile. So my memories of laundry come laden with layers of memories of the camaraderie of womankind and surprising rare sights. The tumour made me take a pride in small achievements. I become quite fierce that at the very least I would still do all the laundry. I realised that I have always loved the smell of fresh laundry; I just never acknowledged the fact. I don't like ironing and sewing.

Christian and I did have some humdinger arguments! But I also knew on that bicycle ride, that no matter how heavenly a place was, it would turn to hell in an instant if he wasn't there, if something were to happen to Christian. We had a few frightening situations and I always trusted Christian's good instincts. If he said, 'we need to get out of here', I didn't question it: just quickly bicycled away. Even if we had been arguing moments before.

Back in London, after the ride through Africa, we made the decision to move to the countryside to give the children a life beyond the confines of the city. We lived apart for three nights a week while Christian went to London to build the business. After twenty years I hated the continuing life apart, I just wanted to be together, not saying goodbye on a Monday morning and hello on a Thursday evening. I began to experience my first anxiety attacks: I suspect the tumour had already manifested itself.

My Friend Honey

When the first baby laughed for the first time, its laugh broke into a thousand pieces, and they all went skipping about, and that was the beginning of fairies.

Peter Pan J.M. Barrie

Honey came to stay in the summer of 1972 and kind of stayed for the rest of her life! We would spend some weeks in England, on holiday from our four year posting to Tokyo. I went and stayed with her in Norway where her father was posted for four years.

Honey was the first friend who breezed in to my nomadic life, whom it was up to me to keep in touch with. I was just thirteen. The last of my five years at five different schools and I was not going to leave this one for four years. New postings no longer meant goodbyes.

We had a bond, as her father was in the diplomatic service and Honey had lived all over the world too. But she had been abandoned by her mother aged eight, saying goodbye in a car park, never to see her again. Her father remarried and had another child. Her father also had a very consuming job. Actually, Honey has her own interesting story to tell as he was high up in MI6. So she loved coming to us who understood the international world and yet we had a close, loving family. My mother, bless her, welcomed her in warmly.

Honey was blonde and pretty, with gleaming white teeth (of which I was always envious, mine were awful and a constant source of teenage angst) with the sunniest disposition despite everything. We quickly fell into that teenage girl friendship that boys simply can't understand and which irritates them. Constant laughing, the sharing of the silliest of things and even our own language (Eggy Peggy) Our wit gelled and we laughed our way through the years.

I've watched Kitty have a similar relationship with a friend and I delight at that carefree fun two females can share together. I know Ellie, Honey's daughter, had it with a friend too. Like her mother, Ellie had a spirit of joy with eyes full of humour.

Inevitably it seems when the relationship is so intense a fall out seems to follow somewhere during the friendship. The stuff of life and events happen. Honey moved to Guernsey and then got divorced. I think I wasn't a very understanding friend throughout that time. I moved up to Cheshire and we grew apart. So Honey and I had a few years of a cooler relationship for a few years but it was never completely broken.

She was godmother to my eldest, Cal, and I was godmother to her daughter Ellie. Just as we were gradually renewing our friendship and getting closer again Ellie became ill with an autoimmune liver disease. She died only four days after her sixteenth birthday.

By the time she was really not well, Honey and I were very close again.

Honey phoned me very early one morning and could hardly speak. 'The doctors have said she might not make it.'

They were exceptionally close; Honey and Ellie. I knew from her hoarse wracked sobs that she had Sorrow tapping on her shoulder and he was very big and dark and she was terrified of where she now had to go.

I drove down to see Honey; Christian, without question, taking over my busy life of four children at four different schools.

There is nothing worse than losing a child. Honesty comes to stay and sits quietly in Tragedy's dark shadow. They enter the room and remain quietly, respectfully observing and no one can avoid them.

That week I slept on the floor beside Honey's bed and held onto her duvet cover so I could feel her first stirrings as she awoke, to be ready as the tsunami of grief would hit her. How to get through that moment, morning after morning, when you don't want to wake up and find the ounce of strength left in you to deal with even lifting your head. Gradually, the minutiae of life play their tiny parts through the day. The morning after Ellie's cremation and funeral were so desperate to deal with. She had physically gone. Honey asked me to give a short reading at the cremation. It was the hardest thing I had ever done.

As the days passed I found my way. What our relationship had been so strongly founded upon, humour.

So gently at first; just a little saying about Ellie that made Honey smile at the memory and then a breakthrough one day months later when for the first time I heard her laugh. I had thought I would never hear that again and I missed it. We were on the phone and she said, 'Oh I really take my hat off to you,' about whatever my piece of silly inconsequential news was. 'Oh,' I said in mock surprise, 'Why on earth are you wearing a hat?'

She spontaneously laughed and it was a lovely sound.

It doesn't make the grief any less though, she had a son who needed her, I know, and but for the act of actually doing it, she would rather have died with Ellie on that day.

Honey's grief is so cataclysmic, so she's careful not to overburden any one of her close circle of friends. I'm the friend who makes her laugh, as I always have done. Other friends play different roles to their strengths.

I knew she would dearly love it if she could take my tumour from me and die for me.

One friend of mine arrived quietly while I was out at my radiotherapy session and planted all my pots with pretty flowers. As spring came through my six-week course of treatment I got such joy seeing the little spring flowers peeping through. I was so grateful.

Everyone played their own part in so many different ways. And if they didn't, I didn't question it.

So that's something I have worried about. Overusing certain friends. Making my tumour something they have to take on. No!

So I learnt from Honey.

All who can will support you to their strengths.

61

I also make no judgments. I get a lot of people saying guiltily to me, 'Oh I'm sorry' if they haven't been in touch for a while.

Don't worry: I understand you all have busy lives.

I didn't get in touch much with a friend for a couple of years after her husband died. I always felt guilty but now I know what a duplicitous form such a deceiving emotion arrives in. When the timing is right or there is something to actually do it will be right: don't force it

When I did ring her it was to suggest we went to New York City to belatedly celebrate her fiftieth birthday. So was formed my NYC girls support group.

Lisa was one of that group. She had trained as a nurse and went on to become a surgical educationalist, a specialist training advisor to the surgeons, in the medical world. She was my 'go-to' person when I needed anything explaining or medical terms clarifying. I called her my demon slayer, for the demons that attack in the night. She would soothe my fears, with practical advice and slay my demons with facts; although how she found any hard facts to be positive about I don't understand. She was always quick to reply to my worried texts and ever patient with my questions putting my fears to rest on the phone. I was concerned about overusing her but there are so many questions you think of after every medical meeting: what did they mean by that, were they saying this, and how I should interpret the medical jargon, that I picked up the phone every time to her because I was frightened and I needed to understand. And every time she somehow managed to slay those demons.

A good friend knows all your stories, a best friend has lived them with you.

Source unknown

Close friends from younger days are also important: Caroline Socha and Nikky Shergold were from my university era and have both remained very constant. Both had difficult childhoods, with broken homes and mothers who all but abandoned them and again my mother welcomed them into our family life warmly. They quietly want to exchange that generosity of spirit my mother gave to them and the warmth of family love. They have leapt into support and help care for me that leave me feeling humbled. They take weeks out of their busy lives and come and do full time care for me.

My advice is if you haven't got your own family, find one who will welcome you in and make you a part of theirs too.

Christian organized a rota of friends for my hospital visits for radiotherapy and chemo. These stalwart friends who drove me long hours out of their busy lives were my link to what had become quite a distant outside world. I relished the gossip and news they would bring. I treated my radiotherapy days as 'spa' days: The journey with friends, lying down with a very tight facemask on and listening to lovely music. The nurses got into the whole music choices I brought. The six weeks flew by.

The rota of drivers also brought picnic lunches and evening meals, giving Christian much needed respite from constantly cooking.

Teaching at The White House School

*We are such stuff as dreams are made on; and our little life
is rounded with a sleep.*

The Tempest Act 4, scene 1. William Shakespeare.

All four of my children went through The White House
Primary School in Whitchurch, Shrophire. I've been
interested in education ever since I was a teenager and I
completed my PGCE Drama Secondary at Manchester
Met University and taught in a sixth-form college for a
while. A tragedy with a child, called Freddy Hall, meant
that at the end of one summer term the children were
facing the cancellation of their annual flagship summer
production. I offered to help stage the production. Helen
Clarke, the head teacher only knew me as a parent but said
yes, anything to keep some sort of normality for all the
children who were having to deal with the loss of one of
their own. Primary schools are tightly-bound communities
with emotions running high at the most normal of times,
let alone a death of a child.

The first day Helen was up on the stage manoeuvering
two large bright yellow plastic box steps around. She was
struggling somewhat and the children were watching her
puzzled.

'What are you doing, Mrs Clarke?' asked one.

'Can't you see?' she replied in consternation, 'I'm
building an ancient civilisation!'

My heart sang. Now this was someone I could work
with! She had creative energy, she just got up and did

things and inspired the children. In seconds every child was busy building an ancient civilisation. I stood up and joined in and never looked back.

Helen gave me such creative freedom in all my drama with the children that I had eight very happy years there. To be in a position to open up young minds and see them gain confidence, explore and develop themselves through drama is an amazing privilege.

As a drama teacher it is possible to have 'magic moments': a synergy, that sees the universal human condition in a moment of theatre - sees into human kind, sees into our souls, in a level that is more than the sum of its moment.

That synergy, where everything collides in one moment and there is a deep understanding of the universal truth. It's so deep that the whole room goes silent and no one breaks the moment. Obviously it's rare as the children are all under twelve and there's inevitably one who puts up their hand as the deep moment is being digested and says, 'Mrs. Lee, I need the toilet!' and the synergy of performance, context and understanding that has created such a compelling atmosphere in the space between us all is broken. I treasured those moments when I hardly dared breathe for fear of breaking the moment. They are rare.

It can only happen when you've 'guided' the children so they get there themselves. It is not a didactic thing. That moment, for example, when Lady Macbeth looks at the blood on her hands and finally realises the enormity of what she has done. But to get those moments you have to allow a certain 'chaos' and tremendous freedom in the space. Allow the chaos and the running off of steam inside the children, and then rein it in carefully pulling out the best. I always had a back-up plan – a get back to the classroom safely option ready.

Health and safety being paramount there were many times Helen would walk in showing visitors around. She would enter beaming and then I would see her face fall in horror as what looked like utter pandemonium was going on with no control. As she got to know my ways, when with visitors she would put her head cautiously around the door looking to see if we were still wild with exploring random ideas or at the calmer constructive stage.

I had teaching assistants and at first their backs were to the wall in the chaos and that I should allow such freedom but they all embraced it and we had a lot of fun. It was very useful having more eyes around the room too. Some wild idea that a child may have which looks extreme can always be brought into the stage space and used but made into a positive contribution. The children took great pride when their ideas were used. What was always particularly satisfying was when a shy child, maybe with little confidence first spoke aloud and began to have assurance.

The only thing I didn't allow were the boys to pretend to have a gun. Not just because of the ethics but a gun in drama is so reductive. It closes everything down. The children were good at keeping to the rule.

I never made a child do something they didn't want to do. Some will be glad never to go on a stage or do drama again. There were always plenty of other things for those children: I relied heavily on a couple of children as technicians all year with the sound system. I needed children I could trust with delicate sound systems, listen and be ready and even pre-empt problems. It was a joy working closely with these children and seeing them realise they were playing a very important part in the team and gaining so much from the responsibility. I was never let down.

It's not about making them arrogant or turning them into little stars it's about giving them a voice.

Drama enables children to discover their voices and theatre to use them.

Drama enables children to explore our challenging, complex and uncertain world in their own terms, offering their own expressions to ancient and modern stories, old and new worlds and to make sense of events, remote and close to their own lives.

Source unknown

I would overhear parents at the door picking their children up and saying casually, 'have you had a good day?'

'Yeah,' the child would reply.

And I would feel my heart beating with achievement: Oh yes they have had a good day; today they found their voice.

One thing I always tried to do was engage the parents into really thinking about what their children could achieve in front of them through drama and make an emotional connection, not just polite clapping, forget it and rush home for tea, their daily duties and tick offs.

My favourite was a short performance piece we put together to commemorate the start of the hundredth anniversary, in 2014, of the beginning of the First World War.

There's a term in drama called 'body as prop' where you use the body to represent something inanimate. Some children used their bodies to create a trench wall while others, on a whistle and a command from a child, climbed out over the top. As they did so I played Beck Smith's version of 'I vow to thee my country'. To see the earnest faces of these young boys, aged ten and eleven, but not much younger than the actual soldiers who died, and then their looks of bewilderment as they acted being mown down was deeply moving.

The girls, with little red crosses on white paper hats emerged to tend to the dying so tenderly, and that's never easy with primary school girls acting with boys. There were no props, no lights, and no costumes, just in their school uniforms. Using the 'body as prop' method the girls formed themselves into pairs and carefully, and with each boy's co-operation, lifted one of the boys up onto their knees as if the boy had fallen down dead after going over the top. Then, each pair of girls, working with 'their' boy, stretched their arms out straight and so 'sculpted' the boy into the shape of a cross. With all the boys being sculpted thus into a long co-ordinated row, it was a profoundly moving and also picturesque scene, and an intensely powerful and moving moment.

At that moment every parent understood that if this had been one hundred years ago this would have been their son. There was such innocence and determination in all their bright little eyes. Just as it would have been, for all those original poor boys who gave their lives.

The parents had to go and have a coffee to recover.

'What have you done to all the drama parents? They were in bits' I was asked all that Open Morning. But I had made them connect and created a moment they hadn't been expecting from a primary school drama. Of course the wonderful music and Beth's gentle, nostalgic version of it helped!

The first drama lesson of a new academic year is a strange gathering. Neither side knows what to expect of a whole new dynamic group of individual children and they eye me tentatively wondering what sort of teacher I will turn out to be. It's often an indicator of how the whole year will progress in drama being such a 'free' exploratory subject. So a lot of care goes into the planning of the first lesson of term and depending on the response whole strategies can change. I was always nervous.

One first lesson I thought had gone 'smoothly' and as we left the studio I heard, 'That was awesome!' Phew! It was going to be a good year with that class. I had my leader who would pull the others up and along with her. It was one of my best classes and they went to tremendous effort to send me an amazing card from them all, personally signed, even though they had scattered to new secondary schools and even Peru.

There's a certain wistfulness in saying goodbye at the end of the summer term when you have shared so much time, development and emotion with a class. But the summer play meant we went out on a high. And I would get home at the end of the last performance elated and down a glass (or two) of Prosecco and wake up on my first morning of post play… already thinking of next year's play!

I wrote three of their summer plays and a winter play and adapted *Peter Pan* from the script at Great Ormond Street Hospital. Helen wrote the music for 'Hoodies and Tutus'. Then a new music teacher, Peter Godfrey, arrived and composed the music for my scripts. It was a great partnership. He has composed film music for me since then.

There is constant writing and adapting of dramas at primary schools and I used the wealth of brilliant published school musicals a lot.

But teaching is relentless, requiring huge energy. And I yearned to go back into film where I started my career. At one Ofsted review he put his head in his hands and said, 'How do you have such energy to keep that going day after day?'

'I have a passion for it,' I replied.

One of my most bizarre magic moments was during an Ofsted inspection observation of me, which are the most frightening of things. It's like someone walking in on your marriage for an hour randomly one day without warning and judging your whole marriage and you by it. We were doing *Romeo and Juliet* and that year Ofsted had a focus for primary schools pushing the potential of gifted children.

All the children had a text adapted for primary school making Shakespeare's language more accessible to them. There was a moment when we were looking at how every adult in the play played their part in facilitating the deaths of *Romeo and Juliet*. I asked the children to demonstrate this through small groups and freeze frames.

Before I even knew it we had a synergy, a magic moment happening as every child realised the adults, who in their own lives are supposed to be protecting them, had betrayed that trust. One by one I saw their faces grasp the concept that as children *Romeo and Juliet* had been let down by the very people who should have been guiding them. And how that impacted on the adults around them in their own lives. The part each and every one of us plays in the events of other people's lives. I held my breath and hoped that magic moment would last to the end of the observation...

'Mrs Lee, can I go to the toilet?'

Then the bell rang.

I found that if I could find just one or two children within a larger class of children who 'got it' then they would pull all the others on side and up into a cohesive positive whole and raise the standard.

I often turned to Shakespeare because he has all the universal themes of life that children can relate to: love, hate, jealousy, envy, greed, compassion, forgiveness, reconciliation and power, which in children's terms is bullying. All part of a child's growing life. Daily play ground stuff that leads onto the adult workplace and who they become as people. You see all the world leaders and politicians in the playground! Shakespeare gave me the opportunity to discuss it through drama and help the children who were suffering to make some sense of it. They play all these themes out in the playground. Throw in a bit of stage fighting and magic and red paint for blood and it always works, well almost always!

I also used Shakespeare a lot in a teenage anger management programme I was involved in. Initial reluctance from the students who have negative memories of school and have generally 'failed' in our rigid academic school system are quickly won over as they see the relevance of his themes in their own lives: jealousy and rage gradually leading the way to understanding why they have behaved so. And then we had the fun part of *A Midsummer*

Night's Dream and a huge lad who had come a long way announcing proudly in a strong Liverpudlian accent, 'Hey, get me! I'm going to play a fairy king!'

But I often felt a complete fraud. I used to think at the end of every term, '*Phew! I got away with it again!*' I never quite shook off imposter syndrome.

I never felt as though as I was a true teacher. Luckily a drama teacher can't wear formal teaching clothes. I used to spend too much of my time sitting on the floor with the children, on my knees or crawling around as we created movement and my 'blacks' were lycra dresses and tights with long colourful scarves (always handy suddenly in a lesson to become a prop or costume that enhanced the scene)

I often chucked my dress on inside out and would arrive at the school to have the secretary's voice sharply behind me, 'Mrs Lee. Inside out!' and I would quickly go and change it round in the staff loo. This would happen even more frequently when I was carting props in for shows because I was in such a hurry. Christian and the family would come to the plays and recognize half the stage set and props were from our house.

Of course at a primary school I did have the most wonderful help from the other teachers, a particularly talented art teacher, teaching assistant set painters, costume makers and there were always one or two right by my side. Theatre is collaboration and I encouraged and welcomed their ideas and couldn't have achieved almost all of it without their constant support and help.

And then you get to that moment when it's all set. This is the work of the year. The parents are there and a child who has been trusted with that job switches off the house lights proudly. An expectant hush falls.

But the studio was where I felt most at ease, a large, bright open space with so many possibilities. No lights or even stage unless put up especially for performances, but you don't need all that. You just need one person in the room, standing there, and the deepest of emotions and drama can be created. Just humans.

On our bicycle ride through Africa, I spent a few days in a classroom in a remote village in Sudan. Kids in Sudan were all barefoot, the classrooms were devoid of all the usual educational wall decorations, and yet there was a real sense of learning, a deep desire to listen in earnest, to get out of the poor confines of the village. Why on earth would you fool around? The teacher, a quiet, diligent man, had put a young boy in the front row. 'He wants to be a doctor.' he said. There were over one hundred children all around him. No stationary. It costs the poorest of families to go to school. It made me wonder about our free 'so cool to fool around at school' and confrontational teacher-pupil culture. I hope he made it and fulfilled his dream.

I'm making it sound as though everything I did was a huge success and feel I'm boasting. Believe me, it wasn't, and I'm not! In the nature of the freedom and experimentation I gave the children, I would emerge sweating from some lessons so grateful Ofsted hadn't witnessed it, as I would have definitely been marked 'inadequate'. How that clock would drag. Even a toilet request was welcomed to give me precious seconds to think. I would feel a failure and that I had let the children down.

'The endless box ticking', made easier by computers but also computers allow it all to become an unnecessarily huge task. This is where Helen was so good with me. She recognized that my default in drama and teaching was 'yes', very rarely 'no' and that I wasn't interested in the detailed careful written assessments demanded by the educating bodies. My strengths were all about the energy of the moment and ultimately the plays and I could easily see how each child had progressed or not. Why the need to write it all down?

And fortunately for me, she allowed that strength to thrive and allowed 'not good' in my appraisal for the written assessment tick boxing.

The paradox and irony is that the teaching profession, particularly primary, is mostly relegated to low-earning females. The alpha jobs of high-earning males are promoted to the financial worlds. But the economy must be strong so it will be forever the same. I could only indulge my passion because I had a husband paying the mortgage and the bills.

It's deeply ingrained in our culture, this foolish idea that teaching is a kind of secondary profession, and this stupid view isn't helped by the equally stupid remark by George Bernard Shaw that those who can do, and those who can't, teach. In fact, teaching is the most glorious and expressive of professions. Besides, there are many different ways of teaching. Millions of composers have learnt technique and inspiration from Mozart and Beethoven and a host of other composers, just as millions of writers have learnt lessons in how to write, and the even more important lesson of why to write, from Shakespeare and Dickens and a vast range of other writers. So does this make Mozart, Beethoven, Shakespeare and Dickens inferior artists? I don't think so.

If I saw a mother trying to get to work on time with a dawdling child, and the mother saying goodbye to her charge with only just concealed relief ('Come on! Mummy's got to get to work!'), it was always that child, particularly the younger ones, who you could expect to appear before you at break or lunch time with a 'tummy ache' and the 'I want my Mummy' and cry quietly. What they had was heartache, nothing to do with the tummy. We are such sensitive beings.

I'm not judging the mothers or fathers with all the stresses of traffic and work and the stuff of life. I probably did it myself too before I saw the effect from the other side. Distraction was always the best. 'Well, you'll love what we're going to do this afternoon!'

But that drop off moment can mean the difference between the child having a good day and thriving, engaging and joining in or being miserable all day because they felt unwanted in the morning. None of us like the feeling of rejection, particularly from those we think will never do it. A child has no control so it's much worse in their little lives.

All of this pedagogy has been written about in great educational and psychiatry studies, but the stuff of life happens and it wasn't until I saw the daily pattern so clearly from the other side that I realised the importance of that moment. But it's the same in adulthood: we just deal with it and hide it, carrying it all day. We have more control to put it right – sending an x on a text or a xx.

Growing up, moving all over the world, my own education had huge gaps. Different countries, different languages, no national curriculum and over five consecutive years between the ages of eight and twelve, I went to five very different schools. I was into survival, not learning. Always the new girl: trying to edge my way in to a long established friendships or groups of girls.

Just at that stage when they are all fighting for their future female hierarchy and the massive friendship makes and breaks happen. And I was not known by the teachers so had to fight my new presence each year. In many ways it set me up for life and was a good thing. But it could be lonely. No wonder I delved down the bed at night and pretended to enter Narnia, or Neverland, where I could control events more in my imagination. Added to which the schools were so eclectically different: a Spanish school in Argentina (where we saluted a Las Malvinas flag every morning in a long ritual before any learning began) a highly academic traditional London school, where I was so far behind I played the tummy ache game instead of looking stupid, then a very rural school where we were allowed to do as we liked and play with the bunnies all day. Then a 2000-strong comprehensive, then an exclusive girls' boarding school designed to turn us into wives and ladies. So I had never heard of long division and who knew what a 'Celt' was? I quietly used The White House School to fill all the rather large gaps in my primary education.

There's no blame or ill feeling. I had such a happy, privileged childhood with a loving family, wonderful mother and father and sisters and got to see the world in a luxurious way. I can't even get close to the catastrophe of the human tide of uprooted children and wonder at the detritus of damage of their tomorrows.

But I craved stability, making a friend that I then didn't have to say goodbye to soon afterwards.

I had my own little box of constant friends made out of card and coloured in: the old fashioned sort you could hang paper clothes on. They each had a name and a character and I lived in their world as much as they were part of mine especially when the upheavals of moving and new schools was happening. One night my toddler sister, Cecelia, came in and found the scissors I had been using to make a new girl. She cut almost every doll into tiny pieces, unrecognizably tiny bits of paper. Not maliciously and she could never have known. She was just delighted not to be stopped in her own form of artwork. The loss I felt was devastating. I even tried to stick some of them back together but soon gave up. The cut pieces were too tiny. I had to move on and maybe she did me a favour.

I started at The White House when Robin was in Reception. The other three had all left for secondary school. Robin had had to literally and metaphorically speed down sand dunes to keep up with us as a family. I enjoyed seeing him at school with his peers, keeping out of his way as much as possible, giving him his own space.

Peter Pan
One of my favourite fictional characters is Peter Pan. We used to go to Kensington gardens when I was a child and I was so fascinated by the statue of Peter Pan that I fell in love with the idea of this boy.

The bronze statue is of a sweet-looking boy playing the pan pipes surrounded by fairies. He can fly, which makes him special and he lives on a wild island where stories and adventures are never far away. I was hooked (excuse the pun) and my addiction fed into my desire to find different imaginary lands and to create my own stories.

When I studied the real-life inspiration that led to his conception, it was with dismay and shock I found the sad news, and it took me a while to get over, that, in a sense, Peter Pan himself committed suicide. Sorry, if that's also new to you and a shock too. It's not strictly accurate. Created by Scottish playwright and novelist Sir J.M. Barrie (1860-1937), Peter Pan, the mischievous boy, was actually an amalgamation of the five Llewellyn boys known to Barrie as a family. Peter (1897-1960) was the third eldest. He threw himself under a tube in Sloane Square in 1960. He grew to dislike having his name associated with *Peter Pan*, which he came to refer to as 'that terrible masterpiece'. The second youngest son, Michael, drowned when he was twenty (1900-1921). The perils and potential tragedies of life are echoed in Barrie's world-famous play.

The story of *Peter Pan* metamorphoses successfully into so many genres and art forms it can withstand pantomime, Disneyfication; it can be performed as a straight play.

Ten little known facts about Peter Pan
1. The very first idea of *Peter Pan* arose out of a tragedy in Barrie's childhood. James Barrie's brother died in an ice skating accident the day before his forteenth birthday. James Barrie was seven years old when he lost

his brother. His mother called his brother: 'My boy who never grew up'.

2. James Barrie met the Llewellyn Davies family in Kensington Gardens. When both their mother and father died, leaving five young boys orphaned, he adopted them. They were his inspiration for *Peter Pan and the Lost Boys*.

   In Barrie's own words Peter Pan and the story was created: 'By rubbing the five of the orphaned Davies boys violently together, as savages do with two sticks to produce a flame. That is all *Peter Pan* is: the spark I got from all of them'.

3. *Peter Pan* was originally written as a play in 1904 and called *The Boy Who Wouldn't Grow Up*.

4. The name of the mythological God playing the flute inspired the name Pan. *Peter Pan* is not described much in the book except that he still has a full set of baby teeth.

5. James Barrie commissioned a statue of *Peter Pan* as a present for all the children of London. They put it up in Kensington Gardens in the night as a May Day children's surprise. There are seven statues from the same mould around the world.

6. James Barrie gave a donation from *Peter Pan* to Great Ormond Street Hospital for Children as early as 1908. He gave the copyright to Great Ormond Street Hospital for Children in 1929 and again in his will. He requested that the amount of money raised from *Peter Pan* should always remain a secret.

7. Great Ormond Street Hospital opened on St. Valentine's Day 1852. At that time it was the only children's hospital in the English-speaking world. For over 160 years Great Ormond Street Hospital for Children has been one of the leading children's hospitals in the world and the largest centre for research into childhood illnesses.

8. In 1987 Parliament proposed, for the first and only time in the history of copyright law, that *all* royalties from *all* performances of *Peter Pan* – amateur and professional, should all be given - to Great Ormond Street Hospital for Children - in perpetuity. Unusually for parliament: this unique proposal was agreed unanimously.

9. Great Ormond Street Children's Hospital did not charge us a license fee for putting on our production of *Peter Pan* at The White House School. They were incredibly open about script adaptations so I went back to the original book for mine. We made more from donations over the run than any other school play had ever done.

10. I played Peter Pan. Robin also subsequently played Peter Pan.

I belong to the Whitchurch Little Theatre Group, an amateur dramatic Society, and some years ago we performed *Peter Pan*. I played Peter and I loved saying those iconic lines. I even flew although the harness was very uncomfortable and dug into my ribs so I had to try not to grimace the whole time I was flying.

Robin played Peter Pan in the school play and he really looked the part, blond and impish, with just the right amount of mischievousness. He had a really feisty Tinkerbell and together they were brilliant.

On Kitty's graduation day, at Oxford Brookes University, the day had gone beautifully and I was so proud and happy for Kitty who glowed with it all. Kitty then took us around the centre of Oxford. As she walked past one narrow alleyway she casually said, 'Oh, there's the lamp-post that inspired C. S. Lewis and the Narnia Stories.' The lamp-post that lit my way through childhood. I walked reverently towards it. It glowed softly just as in that snow covered illustration in the original books. I touched it. I never thought I would find the actual one.

Helen Clarke, my headmistress, has deep faith. After I told her about my diagnosis she was deeply supportive with her messages and sent me little religious quotes and tiny books, tentatively, not wishing to force anything I may not be open to onto me. They were helpful because the language used is deeply comforting, such as 'Be not afraid.' And 'For I will walk with you.' What could be nicer than that in the lonely place I had found myself in? But I told her, 'I am still in negotiations with God!'

I still am.

Almost at once, I had lost all interest in the news. I used to listen to the *Today programme* on Radio Four every morning after dropping Robin by the school bus.

But instead of being a distraction the news had become an irritant. Why didn't they all just get on? At that time Syrian beheadings and other atrocities were pretty much the daily fare. I felt irritated that the people who did these evil and stupid things could choose the course of their lives whereas mine had now been determined for me. Why choose to kill each other when being kind would be so much more fulfilling?

There was one very bizarre moment when as skipping through the radio channels I came upon an old friend from university presenting on air (LBC Radio Clive Bull) It felt like he had just walked in and the years dropped away. Less hair of course! He metaphorically waved at me in passing across the years, his face lit by the bright light of the screen. His programme was news and I wanted music. I turned to Classic FM, soothing and at that time of year lots of lovely life affirming Christmas carols full of hope. The advertisements still told me to 'hurry, hurry, hurry' and get that sofa.

I didn't realise that I would never drive Robin to the school bus again. Our journeys, often very quiet, were punctuated by a sudden deep philosophical discussion about ethics, or the soul. I thought I had several more years of that school run and sometimes used to even wish away the routine of it. Be careful what you wish for.

Facebook

As soon as I was diagnosed I felt differently about Facebook (FB). I had been happy to be a part of FB but I felt now I wanted to remain private. So apart from a couple of quick insignificant posts I dropped away from it all. I would browse and was quite happy seeing everyone else's normal lives. But I didn't want to join in at all.

But FB had other ideas and did, in fact, become a close part of the days in hospital. I suddenly saw posts of support from all around the world, rippling outwards to extended family and friends and their friends. Candles were lit for me in America, South Africa, Australia, Europe and the UK and their warmth resonated from the photos. I was connected around the world during my operation - isn't that an amazing achievement of humankind? And I found I had tremendous support from very many people. Friends and families of different religions around the world were also saying prayers. So I resumed being active on FB.

Then my operation was cancelled.

A patient who absolutely needed the most urgent emergency treatment had been brought to the hospital and quite reasonably that patient was regarded as a more important priority than me.

They brought me food and tea and at that moment I was so weak with hunger and thirst I didn't even think of the consequences of not going for surgery that day.

Rupert arrived and apologized for the delay.

'Did you save his life?' I asked.

'Yes,' said Rupert.

'Well, then that is all that matters,' I replied.

'The thing is,' said Rupert, 'we have a man in with a very large tumour and also we have you, and only one operating theatre, and one High Dependence Unit. So we'll see about tomorrow morning. But if we can't do it tomorrow it'll have to be postponed until after New Year. I'm going on annual leave until the middle of January. I'm sorry,' Rupert said again.

4

SOUL SEARCHING: THE NIGHT
BEFORE SURGERY

Throw your soul through every open door.

'Rolling in the deep' Adele

Facing surgery is a very, very lonely business.

I wanted it completed and all the uncertainty done with. Rupert had run through a list of everything that could go wrong. The worst ones were infection, brain bleed or an epileptic seizure during surgery in which case they would induce coma. But I wasn't fazed by any of these things. I just wanted the operation done.

This is what I wrote on my iphone through the long, lonely hours of the night:

In twelve hours I will know if I am to be operated on. I read for a while, drink tea, sleep a little. But when I check the time again only four hours have passed.

01.00am.

I survey the scene from my large hospital window. It's high up and I look down on the streetlights shining over the glistening wet red roofs and the rain-spattered shining swathes of concrete below, all showing me a view of Stoke, lying in the middle of England. The wet concrete of the brightly-lit round helicopter pad, waiting silently, ready for its next catch. If I hear the rotor blades throbbing and see a helicopter landing then those people, those casualties, go directly into the operating theatres, especially built with exterior access doors for speed for urgent cases. They would take priority over me, rightly so.

If I'm going to lie awake then I will contemplate what Henry Marsh wondered as he operated: *what is the soul?*

I imagine that it is small, baby-like and helpless and that I am rescuing it, lying in the back streets of Stoke. I pick it up gently, it lies in the palm of my hand and I comfort it. I imagine this soul and I will make the journey into the operation together, so desperate am I for company.

01.57 I look at FB and see swathes more support and encouragement. I imagine them, like an ancient army, up on the green hills behind me up in the dark distance, as they wait out the long night, weary, lying together in small encampments with their candles burning. I imagine them like an army of support with so many little camps and I see a new candle formation burning from Kenya. Good I think, the nimble footed are with me.

I plan a strategy: I decide to go into myself to build strength and not find it from all the messages and communications. Now, I have got to realise it's actually just me on my own who has to do this.

I switch my phone off. I have to harden myself to do that. Click, slide, Apple off: so no pings of positive hugs can come winging in. It's a good sleep.

86

02.01 Four hours until pre-operation preparation.

I'm glad to feel again the quiet, far away strength of my FB family and friends who have carried me so far. I realise it's not rejecting their platitudes of support but gathering them all up as sustenance on the long journey that I have to do on my own. It is in the end my journey not theirs.

02.21 I'm happy on my own, nurturing my newly-found soul. Time for a little quiet reflection in these dark lonely hours of pre-dawn with the street lights twinkling in the alleyways below. I reflect then that the soul represents the very deepest part of what it is to be a human individual. And now I see the daily battle these neurosurgeons run, they save lives but they have to leave it to us to save our souls.

02.28 I have a sudden moment of tiredness so I take a rest.

02.40 I'm tempted to turn on FB give them a wave, but I don't. It detracts my energy, I am stronger for being alone. I know they are all still there. Out there on those dark, damp middle England hills with candles lighting the pre dawn air. They're there in my mind and give me plenty of warmth for the next few hours.

02.44 Just over three hours to go. I must rest. Silence. No rotors bringing emergency surgeries to be undertaken.

05.11 That was a restorative deep sleep. I look out of my large window and see that it has stopped raining. It's peaceful outside over the roads of the dark twinkling city and most others else will wake up to a normal day. Rupert will be getting up soon.

How shall I carry my new little soul? I decide I will place him in a protected nugget of perfect balance towards the back and base of my brain, exactly where Henry Marsh was searching around with his instruments and forming his own questions and theories about our souls. I think now my soul doesn't belong in our hearts. Souls are nothing to do with our blood supply system or pumping veins. Quite separate. I want to place him in the centre of my whole being, who we are. That is his rightful home not flopping about inside the pudding of a beating heart, clinging on wildly, madly being bumped about through life. He's found his rightful place perfectly. I can feel his joy with my decision and he will be good to carry there. I suddenly realise this little bundle has been beside me, with me, all my life and I carried it all this way and never really said hello or even acknowledged its presence.

05.22 My pre-operation nurse is a tall, Asian male, called Fenish, with a smartly trimmed moustache, who stands very straight and dignified. He arrives with my operation gear. He has purple epaulets on each shoulder and a very smart white crisp ironed jacket with neat buttons. Badges of honour and service and little instruments of aid in his pockets. He gives me a clean pressed gown to wear and some protective anti bacterial shower cream, to douse away all the potential bugs that may fly in and give me an infection. He leaves the room. I rather enjoy the pre-operation ritual.

I pamper myself in the long hot shower over-indulging in the strawberry protective anti bug cream. I wash slowly and carefully, leaving no part for ghastly winged bugs to sneak their way in. I clean my teeth and use mouthwash, in case there is already one lurking in there rather too close to my brain waiting to make its attack.

I take pleasure in tying the bows of the gown. I look in the mirror and satisfy myself that it is neat. Dignity is very important.

05.53 Fenish arrives again. We do some pre-health checks. Blood sugar, blood pressure. He's quietly preparing everything else: the bed with new clean sheets, removing the towels, tidying. He knows exactly how to prepare perfectly. He doesn't make small talk or chat but is attentive and deferential. He offers advice if I ask. I almost wish I could take him with me but we always have to say goodbye to everyone and be on our own in the end.

06.00 Katya, who has a soft voice and gentle manner, comes and gives me my tablets with quiet encouragement. The final part of getting ready is the protective socks, trickier to get on but good protection against blood clots. Katya hooks me up to my fluids.

I metaphorically pick up my soul and gently place him as my companion within my brain. The winter solstice is over and the days are getting lighter from today. I see it as a good omen for me. I am strong and ready. I have my little soul tucked up safely with me. He's very quiet, making sure he doesn't do anything to disturb me. I know he has settled in well. We are comfortable together already.

06.48 Dressed and protected. Fluids. Checks. Ready.

06.53 Good luck to us my little resting soul and I. You are so quiet I think you must finally be sleeping. I looked for you all over the world and you were right with me all that time. I was looking in the wrong places obviously. You were never that far away but it's up to us to find you, you can make no sign, not even the squeak of a calling baby. Souls say so much, yet they are silent.

09.00 But I didn't go down to the operating theatre. A nurse entered and was surprised to see that I was still in my room, as though dressed up for an operation party and had accidently been left behind, 'Ooh love, not gone yet? Oh dear. I'll see if you can have a cup of tea.'

I was given a CT scan to check my tumour growth and then thought that I would be sent home until sometime in mid January.

Rupert – The Innkeeper
10.00 I've just heard that Rupert has requested the emergency operating theatre to be opened. They wheeled me down the long corridors, down in the lift to a subterranean world. It was like the set of a James Bond movie. Except that everyone was very friendly to each other and there was such a diverse mixture of accents and languages.

Rupert had worked hard, pulling in an anaesthetist who was on Christmas leave, asking him to leave his own family for me. A Croatian gentleman, he bicycled in across the city of Stoke, to the place where the blue lights flash brightly above the towers of the hospital in this eastern part of the city to do his duty of care: like one of the ancient kings paying homage and bringing his own special skills, wisdom and mixes of myrrh from about 2000 years ago.

Rupert played the part of kindly resourceful innkeeper, finding me a stable when all the inns were full. I chatted to the anaesthetist until the cool liquid was injected into my blood.

It's nearly Christmas Eve, December 22 2015. I had been listening to carols. The story of the nativity is the one of the best stories, illustrating the kindness of humanity that is evident when we collaborate. So that's why I call Rupert the Innkeeper, he found a room when they were supposedly full. The one possibility to redeem all human kind's stupid mistakes in a new little life, to start again with a baby who represents hope and joy, the possibilities of peace and most of all love. Come, little soul. Take my hand. You're very quiet but I feel I have got to know you quite quickly. Come little soul and show me more of your little wise ways. It seems now having thought I rescued you in my longest night, that actually all along it is you who are rescuing me.

I believe SOS – Save Our Souls is not the right cry, it should be SOB: Save our Bodies. Because souls will go upwards, not drown in the sea with their host body. They will fly out and up and then wing themselves free. And they will carry on being souls in the atmosphere never too far from earth because that is their destined ether. This is about the millions of humankind who have either found their souls or who haven't. Nothing ever disappears.

I once went to a music concert, given by Adele, ever an example of a really brightly shining soul who knows its place in her body, so much so that Wembley had its biggest audiences ever. 98,000 people filled the stadium around her. Now that is a very strong soul. As she sang, 98,000 bright little points of light from mobile phone torches floated around in unison. As though all the souls in their earthly bodies who had found them, had come to listen to the poetry and music and wisdom coming from that one leading good soul in the middle of the huge stadium. Pity the people who have never found their souls and missed this get together! At the end of the evening hundreds of thousands of tiny white papers fluttered down as though gentle snowflakes were falling. One landed on my head. It had a message on it.

'Throw your soul through every doorway'

Souls will fly free once their earthly body can no longer look after them. But they are still the same soul. I believe our soul is the empathy in our humanity.

I don't believe that saying 'He had an evil soul'. He just didn't have one at all. Souls are not evil. You either have your soul or it's missing from you so you have no empathy. You cannot become part of the great-shared souls of humanity. As soon as you find your soul, however late in life, it looks after you. It brings empathy with it as its gift. Its home is your body, its nourishment is music, dance and poetry, maths and science of our world.

As a small female my default protection in life has been to look for kindness in men's eyes. Their souls shine a little light through and tell you they are there. On our bicycle ride through Africa we had a few tricky incidents, one arrest, mostly overzealous border guards hoping for a bribe. Until I was in front of someone and I could see their soul peeping its presence through from behind their eyes, then I knew we were safe and everything was going to be all right. But with the ones who hadn't got their souls nestling safely inside them, there was no hope for us for any negotiations: the bribes had to be paid.

The spectrum of humankind around the planet is so diverse; people are so different and yet our humanity remains a constant. People who have found their souls can empathise across languages, cultures, humour and care. Cycling through Africa taught me that.

Anyone involved in ordering or committing genocide is without their soul: That's why they can do it. No soul is present there.

Yet the experiences we encounter in life can make it very difficult for a soul to protect itself from deep damage.

My family was from the silver spoon brigade but those silver spoons are sometimes poisoned on the underside. When my uncle was a young boy, he begged to be able to keep one kitten from a litter that had been born on the farm. He was desperate. I saw the tear-stained letter he wrote, aged seven, sent from his austere boarding school hundreds of miles away across the African bush.

A small boy craving something to love at a school where there almost certainly was none and abuse the norm. His father, of that stiff upper lip, man-up generation, killed them all so when the boy arrived home with excitement it turned to dismay and shock. Years later when we were staying with him, Caroline, Jacky and I were playing in the garden. We were about seven, five and three, the ages when fluffy kittens for young girls are heavenly.

He brought a litter of kittens out in front of us. He stopped us in our eager tracks and before our eyes first drowned them in a bucket of water and then smashed every one of their heads against the wall: the cutest of kittens turned into blood and guts and death. It was actually too much for us to take in. I buried the memory deep. It was only when I saw his childhood pain through his letters home from school that I began to understand the circles of life. So his soul was always there. It had struggled through inflicted damage, but he had held onto it. He had a soul but it couldn't cope with the damage inflicted on it. He committed suicide by drinking acid. One of the most painful and slowest of deaths.

I think that's the struggle so many people and their souls have to deal with throughout their lives: fighting against the damage done.

So there you are, Henry Marsh, those are my pre-brain-surgery thoughts on what you began in your chapter on the soul, in your book *Do No Harm*, from the other side of the table, you looking in on the rational side, I on the brain-operated side of irrationality.

5

THE NIGHT OF THE BRAIN SLAYERS

There's a divinity which shapes our ends
Rough hew them how we will.

Hamlet Act V scene 2 William Shakespeare

Post surgery

When I was wheeled out of the lift I saw Christian and my four children. They were all looking at me expectantly as though I might not recognize them, that in some way brain surgery would have changed my personality. So I called them all by name, and reassured them all I was still 'me'.

They later told me that before I emerged from the lift after five hours of brain surgery, the family had been waiting by the wrong lift. Suddenly, a tiny, very old, white-haired lady was wheeled out. *Good God,* they all thought, *what has the surgeon done to Mum?* I was then wheeled out of the adjacent lift to find my family with that nervous laughter you get in heightened situations.

Hooked up to several machines I was wheeled into a room on my own, not HDU, but with a high level of observations.

I said goodbye to the children and then to Christian. I felt too tired to be lonely, although I wished he could stay.

I pretended to be altruistic and encouraged him to go and see a film with the kids. It had been a hard day for all of them too. I had spent most of it asleep.

There's that strange feeling of wistfulness when the last familiar face walks out of your room. If I had not been tied to so many machines and been able to, I would have jumped up and said another farewell.

I had learnt that preparation is everything. To try and foresee all that lies ahead that could conspire against you. Robert Falcon Scott was only eleven miles from safety and food storage after a 1,700 mile trek there and back to the South Pole: it was prolonged bad weather which did for him and his friends. They say the journey down Everest is more dangerous than the climb up, when spirits are buoyed with the dream of the achievement ahead. That photo of Scott and his team at the South Pole knowing they have been beaten in their race is etched with disappointed faces. That can't have helped the weary journey home. Maybe they didn't want to arrive back with a feeling of failure.

But I was not prepared for these imaginary crawling creatures of the night. Post-brain surgery, I had no defence ready for the tricks the brain plays on itself. I shall call them the brain slayers because that's how they appeared to me. Their favourite food is fresh post-surgery brain meat and they inflict their greedy damage through the night. Even before you see them you can hear they are going to take big slurps, and there's nothing you can do to stop them. I could not move and they can easily see a fresh victim inside the large dark windows.

As darkness falls they start flitting in, darting under cover away from the nightlights of Stoke as they snap on.

Keeping out of any light, they flit closer and closer until you can hear their claws and beaks hitting the windows. Rupert's kind face appears in my head as if to warn me.

The brain slayers have a hollow, hissing squawk that seems to laugh at me and shake my brain. We're coming to eat your brain and we are all powerful. *Caw! Caw! Caw!*

They mock their helpless, prone victims. They screech as they, the brain slayers thump at the black windows, frenzied in their time slot of darkness to claw their way in to the fresh brain juicy matter; newly ravaged by surgery; fresh meat and the possibility of crunching a soul. They are dreadful creatures who fly through the trees and on the hills around where my FB supporters are camped with their candles. The brain slayers hate the candles and streetlights. They like to keep to the darkest of dark places. They are constant in their timings, darkness brings them out so winter is their active time of long feasting. They hit the windows repeatedly trying to find ways to slither in.

There are two nurses on duty for me, one very young and pretty, with neatly coiled hair and a pristine uniform, the other, much older, with dyed red hair and a hard line of a mouth: she has done this night shift before many times. But crucially they are not High Dependency Unit nurses. I am one of four patients under their care.

I doze and keep hearing the brain slayers' attempted violation of my room. Scritch, scratch, screech, their claws on the frames.

I am ravaged with thirst. My brain feels as though it has become hot dry ash and I want to pour cool water through it to calm it down. I press the bell in my hand. I can't raise my head or sit up. There are still two cannulas in me, and all sorts of other wires around. I couldn't move even if I wanted to; it feels like my brain is raw, dried out, perfect for the brain slayers to crunch.

It feels like forever before my bell call is answered. The young nurse snaps on the overhead strip lights and my brain nearly explodes with the pain of the brightness. I cry out.

'I'm thirsty,' I whisper.

She disappears without a word and comes back eventually with a jug of water and an open cup. She puts it down hard on the tall table beside me and turns immediately and leaves the room. Not a glance or a kind word.

I stretch to reach either the cup or the water jug. I can't reach either and even if I could I wouldn't have the strength to lift and pour and then if I managed that how would I drink it lying flat?

This is the work of the brain slayers. This is how they win: they delve into the nurses and use them to weaken us.

I buzz again and wait ages. They are busy as they walk by, my door is ajar. Eventually a nurse comes in.

'I can't reach,' I whisper, politely.

She pours a cup full and pushes it towards me and walks out without a word. I lift the cup and try and sip. The water dribbles all over me. Cold. But I get some down and feel relief.

My two nurses come in and do blood pressure and other checks through the long night. Each time they snap on the bright lights and I jerk with the shock of the brightness.

Eventually, I pluck up courage and say, 'Could you please just give me a warning about the lights coming on?'

'Just doing my job,' she replies irritably.

But she does warn me the next time and still snaps it on.

Damn you, brain slayers, trying to get me through thirst and blinding light.

Much later I need a pee. I really don't want to buzz. When it feels like I'm bursting I finally do so. I have lain politely and quietly through all their checks. I don't want to make things worse for myself. I long for the dawn when the brain slayers will slink away. I ache for a friendly, kind word, just something to feel I am a human being with a morsel of dignity even in the physical state I am in. I wish Christian would suddenly walk through the door.

Eventually my buzz is answered. The older nurse, rather gruffly, hands me a cardboard bedpan and leaves the room. I look at it; my brain can't even work out which way it should go. I think I try the wrong way. For fifty-five years my body has been told not to wet in bed and then suddenly I am telling it to do just that.

I lie there all strapped to the wires and wonder how to physically get my self onto this cardboard box while prone on my back. I'm so desperate I hurry the shuffling. It gets squashed and ends up not quite underneath me. I pee all over the bed, all over me. Brain slayers: how low can you stoop?

I buzz.

I allow myself my first tiny morsel of self-pity because I think anyone lying in their own wee and unable to move is allowed to cry.

I once came across a drunk, very disabled man on Westminster Bridge lying in his own urine. He couldn't move. I called for help but the sight of him unable to move out of his own toxic waste left a strong impression. Now here I was at the capricious whim of 'my guards' who may or may not come and clean me up.

I buzz again, really frightened this time of old nurse whose mouth will harden into an even thinner line of fury.

'I'm sorry,' I tremble.

'Why didn't you buzz earlier?' she demands, definitely angry.

'I did.' I'm terrified.

The brain slayers are winning through humiliation.

'No, you can't have done. I didn't hear it.' She snaps, absolving herself of responsibility and leaving me feeling like a small child who has been wrongly accused. It's been a long night. She walks out fast, flicking the flimsy curtain. The more irritated they are, fed up and tired with their long nights of endless requests, the harder they flick the curtain. This flick nearly took the curtain off its hangers.

I was left like a small child trying to redeem myself, lip trembling.

I lay in my own mess for what seemed like a long time.

I had visited Auschwitz just two weeks before.

That's where I had been with Lisa when I had said everything is fragile, it can all turn on a sixpence. My brain now merged that visit, and it was something I had thought about with a horror and anguish ever since, with the reality of where I now found myself. I begin to imagine that I am in Auschwitz, a degraded prisoner with a female prison guard with no soul because the brain slayers have got them and eaten them whole in one victorious slurp. They say the female prison guards in Auschwitz were the cruellest ones:

100

their souls completely extinguished. So I feel the brain slayers are nearly there with me too.

And then as I feel myself falling into the brain slayers' greedy grasp, the two nurses strip everything off me and give me a bed bath.

They expertly roll me out of the wee-soaked sheets and my cotton gown, avoiding all the needles still in my arms. I lie naked on the bare bed. I anticipate irritated roughness at this extra work I have given them to do. I expect to be demeaned although in my mind I am at my lowest: The brain slayers have cradled in and sent me to a concentration camp where they can chew to their darkest content.

But instead I find the warm, soapy sponges are gently massaged over my skin all over, no trace of wee left, efficient but not unkind. And then they root through my wash bag and find a bottle of perfume, Jo Malone, and spray it over me, rather caringly. No Auschwitz guard sprayed perfume on their victim, especially with such care.

I feel as though I am being physically moved from the grim road of humiliation and death through to a tranquil safety and care of a beauty parlour. I open my eyes and don't see Auschwitz guards, just the two dedicated, tired faces of the night nurses. The long hours of the night etched in the creases of their skin. Some of the hair of the young, pretty nurse has escaped its neat coils as though she has had to wipe it all back to help her through the night.

They bring a whole set of new bedding and I've no idea how but seem to gently roll me this way and that, still avoiding the needles place a fresh gown over my head. They bring a bowl for me to clean my teeth.

We three are quite silent, all relieved that the twinkling lights outside the black windows are one by one snapping off as dawn brings a surge in spirits. We have each in our own way survived the night of the ferocious brain slayers. They flutter with angry flaps away because as each light snaps off they know it is the end of their feasting. They slurp their still greedy lips content in the damage they have inflicted, even if they are not sated.

In the months before my diagnosis my father fell onto my mother at their home in Eridge, near Tunbridge Wells, knocking her over and breaking her leg. In one fall he had wiped out his principal carer, and we were jettisoned into full time care for two people. While it was all being set up my three sisters and I took turns helping keep everything going. I had hardly seen my mother's body naked ever in my life, let alone washed her. I loved doing it. She had to sit at the sink with her leg in plaster from toes to hip. So I massaged her back with the warm, soapy sponge and tried to give each muscle care. She had done this for me as her baby. It felt a privilege to do it for her in the circles of life. I was quite put out when a very efficient social services carer arrived and insisted she took over. She was expert at sink washes, whereas I dribbled the water everywhere but there was no love in her hands.

My mother is of the generation who, when my father knocked her over, it was into a lavender patch. She lay there waiting for the ambulance and thought, 'Well, I can't just lie here and do nothing!' so she weeded the lavender bed as far as she could reach.

6
SURVIVING THE BRAIN SLAYERS

'What day is it?'
'It's today,' squeaked Piglet.
'My favourite day,' said Pooh.

A.A. Milne

The day passes quietly. Things all feel so peaceful, after the tough battles of the night. The nurses are all jolly, friendly and upbeat. My surgery has gone well. The family visits briefly but I am exhausted so rest all day.

Neurological wards at night aren't the quietest of places. Patients shout due to their brains not working properly, they wail, they moan, and of course nurses go round taking blood pressure and trying to quieten disturbed people. The second night after surgery is going to bring another night of the brain slayers. I'm already nervous by dusk. I can feel them beginning to stir, to flit. Flicking their wings at the staring black windows. I need to summon strength. They nearly won last night. I dread seeing the two nurses who seemed to be used by the brain slayers. I now have knowledge of the whole existence of this enemy rather than last night's complete surprise attack but I still haven't prepared my defence. Preparation is key. I know now. Preparing against the loss of control again. The big things go but accepting that making a tiny decision brings a huge feeling of freedom, so vital for the self-dignity of humankind.

And then again it is all done for me. I don't have to fight on my own. I am moved to a shared ward and beside me there is Nancy with the face and aura of an angel. I find the secret to bearing the brain demons is to be close to people like Nancy. They provide strong armour against the brain demons who cannot flit their way in at all past the good aura her soul radiates around her. I chat to her and feel comforted. She's eighty-six and has a kind round face and is very calm. The wrinkles on her skin radiate wisdom, a life well lived. She is the youngest of twelve children and all her siblings have died.

But I hear the brain slayers do their ravaging work that night on three other poor patients through the long hours of feasting. I have some earplugs from the afternoon MRI scan. I push them in and their screams of torment muffle. The nurses cope with gentle banter, their own form of armour, as they work endlessly through the night.

A male victim of the brain slayers turns his violent torment outwards, a particularly cruel trick the slayers have, and the female nurses cannot cope. They call for male back up. They need powerful physical strength against these slayers. And still they do it with care and concern never giving in to the depravity of behaviour of the slayers. Controlled strength to contain, not inflict more harm. The two women calling out in anguish turn the torment in on themselves; one of them, I hear the nurse report, breaks some of her own teeth.

As dawn breaks and the town lightens below my window, I see the shadows of the brain slayers flitting away on the outskirts of the city and I know I have won the night battle with complete success. They didn't even bother to attempt one swoop at me. But then I was cradled in the protective armour of Nancy's calm aura, in the bed beside me. I just looked at her peaceful face and felt strength. She was my Dorothea Brook. (See the preface)

At six am. a nurse switches some morning lights on. A helicopter engine roars into life outside as though whooshing away the last of the slinking brain slayers, savagely winging their way full of their anguished feasts. The nurses begin their rounds. We gently say our pleasantries and there is an unspoken palpable togetherness that we have all made it through the night again, even if we did hear the work of slayers so close by.

7
GOING HOME FOR CHRISTMAS

*And all the world was filled with peace and joy
and love and hope.*

Carol4aCure Nativity Play Gillian Lee

I love the anger and ferocity of the rain clattering on the windows as though thousands of demons are trying to get through the glass that had withstood the onslaught and defended me. And the wind in the night, as though welcoming me back to a festival of wildness, letting me know I am still alive; not for me a calm sunny welcome in the post winter solstice day of mid-winter but a wild, fierce, positive welcome, that I relish with its strength of force and the morning blue-sky day full of new possibilities.

It's a shock to find I cannot walk, a right I'd assumed I'd had since my first steps. It will take time but I will walk again.

The tea boy remembers I like ginger biscuits!

Time to check in at last again with the FB supporters. As I arrive I realise the intense support and vigil they have kept for me all through the long days and nights. They have re grouped and massed, connected in different camps and shared the same candles across the world. From Australia and Kenya, to the USA, Europe and South Africa I thank them metaphorically waving up to them all in the hills stretching far around me.

Thank you, FB family. I'm not ready to speak to you all yet, just to wave my gratitude up to you all. They are now packing up their candles and camps, having kept steadfast vigil through my critical hours, leaving messages as they go. I feel nostalgia for the dissolution of the power of their togetherness. They will go on now to happier posts. Frivolous, fun, quotes, stuff of politics and issues they feel strongly about, their outings and excitements and dinners and I will enjoy seeing all of them. But it was a wonderful moment when they all came together, in layers of those who are known me, and layers of their friends and children's friends, countries and continents united. What does that say for humanity? As one in support for me with their comforting messages flying my way. A feeling of wistfulness comes over me as I see them metaphorically leave, although I know they are still all out there really.

Rupert suddenly appears. The good news is that he got eighty per cent of the tumour out. My right leg will get stronger. He doesn't want to go into medical detail although I fire questions at him. I wish him a very happy Christmas and holiday. I like the way he slips neatly and quickly from brief teddy bear kindness into focused efficient neuro surgeon. I know where I am and I like that.

The last needle is taken out.

The rotors hum twice outside but don't thump. The bright red and yellow helicopter looks like a child's toy. Benign, it a symbol of help not dark a dark throbbing threat to my chances of getting home for Christmas.

So begins the slow process of learning to walk again. I see it all from my father's perspective, he is ninety-one, and I am shuffling in his manner. Just to contemplate the marathon of getting dressed to having breakfast seems like a mountain to climb ahead. To get to the bathroom is a journey.

Dizzy, set back, no, just very low blood pressure, drink. Rest.

Warm healing waters of showers! Pampering luxury shower gel wash from a filming shoot abroad from my old life, which really is so far away. But how I enjoy my first sitting shower in 'Ma's style', confident with all the holding bars around me.

I get dressed, which exhausts me and I need to rest.

I spray myself with Jo Malone perfume. Jo Malone breezes easily between my old and new life.

John Lennon's 'So this is Christmas' plays:

Let's hope it's a good one, without any fears.

Yes, let's hope so.

I'm careful to make all the texts I send upbeat. They make me sound fine and I use humour. The truth is my head is broken and very sore. I still have brain cancer. I have a haircut from hell! My body is not really working, I am weak, there is still a long road to travel ahead of me and I will miss out on good times and get cantankerous and full of self pity. I imagine myself in the scene that haunted me from the film *Never Let Me Go* where Keira Knightley's body is broken with surgery. In Henry Marsh's book, the lady left paralysed was the one I remember feeling most sorry for and I have escaped that, at least so far.

It's been the most wonderful journey too so far and who would ever have thought that? I will make strategies to cope with the future.

I think back to me in my £49 Mango dress, partying in London, quite the lady about town. Only I didn't have the energy to change, even into the sparkly cardigan, so I just went in jeans and old boots and was served champagne for the last time. Farewell bubbles.

A hard tack

The right-hand side of my body is very weak. I'm learning to walk again. I will have to pass tests, notably the stair test, to get home. The stair test is one I had prior knowledge about. Before they will give you a discharge letter you have to successfully complete 'The Stair Test'.

It surprises me how important my Christmas means to the staff. I know they want to clear the wards but it's their personal goal. It's been promised to me and they want to succeed.

I used to race a Sigma 33 keelboat in Abersoch in the summer. Jemima, one of the crew on board and a physiotherapist, as we came up to a tack used to urgently call, 'We've got to make this a good one.'

I imagine she is there, winching in with me! Sailing this listing yacht, it will be hard to do that. I'm determined to make it round this race mark.

I'm first on 'physio' list of the morning. Thanks to Mum I know what to do: good leg leads up, bad leg leads down.

I gather strength, imagine Jemima calling the tack and I do it! My leg, inert until that moment, jerked into action! All the staff, dressed as Elves, Snowmen and Santas up and down the corridor, cheered me. It was a surreal sight. I climbed one stair and then another one.

This is a text I sent to Graham, a sailing friend, in reply to his question, 'How are you feeling?

Thank you. Well - like I'm lying in the water leeward side of a crash tack with the windward side looking physically tough and high above my head but my spirit is determined to get there - and the support from everyone feels like I am having my life jacket lifted up out of the heavy water! Hopefully as a sailor that gives you a pretty good idea!

I'm going home to watch my children open up their Christmas stockings, which is the best present to me in the whole world.

That old demon rejection has gone.

My little soul sitting perfectly balanced in the nape of my neck nods his tiny head.

I'm waiting for my tablets and for my letters of discharge.

I start planning where we will go when we travel again. This time I'll travel with metal in my head, and have to face those demeaning tests to prove that I am not a terrorist, guilty before innocent. I can always have that rather surprisingly pleasant massage.

Waiting.

Christian arrives in the ward to take me home on Christmas Eve to my family. It's a slow walk through the hospital corridors and then by lift out into the long-term car park. It's always very bleak on the way home, not on the way out, on holidays. That's how it feels now as I emerge into it from the cocoon of warmth and light and briefly feel a frightening new world around me.

With my new little soul safely stored inside my head. I'm finally bringing him home on Christmas Eve.

8
LIVING WITH DYING. NOT DYING WITH LIVING

What will you do now with the gift of your left life?
Snow Carol Ann Duffy

I am certain that Baloo knew I was ill before I did. He would come and rest his head on my lap and look searchingly at me, his large brown eyes sorrowful. But I had no idea why and just thought he was being affectionate in his maturing years. So I felt such anguish when one dreadful weekend the following January we gave Baloo away to a new home. I couldn't cope with him, he's a large energetic, very strong dog who needs a lot of exercise. Christian was away in London for four days a week and it fell to me to walk him. He was too strong for me on the lead. So we found him a new home. Baloo is very happily settled in his new home with James, who regularly sends us updates and photos. But I still miss him.

We were called back to the hospital frequently during the next year. It was in one of those sessions I was told that I would never drive again, 'our GBMs rarely get their licences back' my oncologist told me. You have to have the medical all clear for a whole year and I will never achieve that.

113

I had to have a very tight facemask fitted for radiotherapy and then daily sessions for six weeks of radiotherapy, for chemotherapy right through from February until September, three-monthly MRI scans with bloods taken and then the results.

At the end of chemotherapy, after my body had recovered, I felt well. Life was getting back to normal at last, I was even managing to work a few hours some days back at Knew Productions making films. My colleague, Richard, had been gentle and understanding and allowed me the rest I needed during the heavy days of chemotherapy. He kindly gave me editing work that I was able to manage and do, which offered me fulfilment and helped me to feel welcomed back into the normal world again.

But the three-monthly scan results were always an anxious time. We would wait nervously in the corridor with hope for good news that it was 'stable'; and stable was the best I could wish for.

Except one month, sixteen months later it wasn't. But it didn't show up on the scan. The scan at the beginning of May 2016, was 'stable' but by mid June it had returned, growing aggressively. It revealed itself to me with two epileptic fits, both of which were very frightening and I went in to hospital. The first one they thought was for a number of reasons, there's always the chance of epilepsy post brain surgery, hence no driving. But with the second one they did a CT scan, which showed 'small but significant growth'. She told me straight away. It was my worst fear. Regrowth. I had hoped somehow to be lucky and to defy statistics, and for it not to regrow as they had assured me it would. But they were right. No matter what I did I couldn't escape, they knew that. Not for nothing is it the most challenging and deadly kind of brain tumour, the most difficult to treat and with the shortest life prognosis.

We were called in to meet Rupert again and he advised a second operation. The tumour was growing so rapidly that soon it would be entwined around the main motor cortex and then he wouldn't be able to get at it without severely affecting my movement. He had it all arranged for the following Thursday. Just the pre-operation tests to do, which we did there on that day and then flew that night to Venice and had the most magical weekend. We had asked Rupert if it was safe to fly and he said yes because I was on such a high dose of steroids. It was our thirtieth wedding anniversary.

The operation was weirdly *déjà vu*, with two differences. I had to drink a liquid that tasted rather as I imagine battery acid would. Then they put a towel over my head to cut out the light as the liquid made my eyes super-sensitive. This was a new mapping technique recently developed that meant they could get as much of the tumour as possible without damaging the nerves. The other difference was I had my own one-to-one critical care nurse and unit, so no night of the brain slayers. It was remarkably peaceful. I don't know if it's because there are more daylight hours, so the brain slayers can hardly begin their feasting and tormenting, but the wards and rooms were much quieter this second time around. It's very peaceful through the short night.

The same stair test, only this time I was kept in an extra day. And a longer recovery. No radiotherapy this time, any more would be counter-productive. But I would have six more months of chemotherapy.

They have made progress with brain tumours, but it's slow and mostly trial stages.

The COC
I am on a trial with the Care Oncology Clinic based in Harley Street, London. It involves taking a protocol of off-label drugs: common well-known drugs but prescribed against cancer. They haven't reported on their findings yet.

Diet
So much has been written about what to eat and what not to eat. From my perspective it all became very confusing and food became my enemy: I blamed something I had eaten in excess for giving me the tumour. Only what was it? Too many carbohydrates? Too much sugar? I thought I had a pretty healthy diet, I have eaten vegetables and fruit every day, chicken and fish. I tried the ketogenic diet but lost too much weight.

Every time the newspapers extolled the 'miracle' cancer curing properties of one particular food, another one ridiculed it. I tried tumeric, berberine, green tea grown in a certain area in Japan, numerous vitamins, Reishe mushroom drops and fish oil. I have no idea if any of these did any good but in the end a grade four GBM is a beast that needs the big guns of surgery, radiotherapy and chemotherapy, until we find something else, an actual, effective cure. So I am not going to advise on diet or supplements.

There are plenty of online forums and discussion groups out there. But be careful: in a vulnerable, clutching-atstraws state you will try anything and believe anyone who gives you hope of life. On the other side are the evidence-based, trialled and proven drugs and treatments recommended by the oncologists. Sometimes it can seem as though they are at war with each other so vehemently do they dismiss each other. This is not helpful for us wounded caught in No Man's Land, with each side saying the other side is the enemy. In the end it is up to me to navigate a path to health, or at least one that gives me the best chance of it. So I have mixed healthy supplements, with a trial, with NHS standard treatment. I have found my medical team to be supportive of the trial I am taking part in.

I had viewed myself as someone who couldn't be hypnotised. How wrong can you be? Fray has come to my house for weekly sessions ever since that day he first met us by chance in hospital. He takes me to a peaceful and beautiful place where physical limitations play no part and the world is made of my memories of good times. I particularly like to have a session with him before scan results, which is always an anxious time. I can even fly when I am hypnotized and I travel to exotic warm places. But my home is England. My England, in the middle of its green hills, I am very English. We become part of the land; we love our places, so of course it's suddenly clear why from ancestral times to the present we fight for our own patches. We fight for them and die for them and then when we are ill we are protected in the lie of the land and we wrap ourselves inside their homely familiar soil.

Orion the giant will still gently glide his steady westerly way across the night sky. I used to watch him follow me from the aeroplane most of the journeys around the world, particularly Tokyo to the UK where I felt he was my sky guardian as my sisters and I flew back to the UK for another term at boarding school, leaving our parents far away in the east.

Where I live now the there is a window above my bed. I leave the blind up and wait for Orion to trek his way past, just checking that all is well, like Roald Dahl's kindly BFG (Big Friendly Giant). Another childhood constant, still there.

I have four grown-up children who make the world a brighter place for me and for others too.

I'm going to listen to music every day and enjoy playing with my new soul.

The gift I have been given is the chance to enjoy living with everything that cancer brings with it. But why did I wait to get a diagnosis of cancer to make me value the moment as much as I now do? The preciousness of the moment. So I will say to you: don't wish time away, don't wish for that exhausting toddler time to end. It does end, and all too quickly. When the children were very young I was given this advice, these ten points below and I'm going to pass them on to you if you have children:

Give them time
Give them unconditional love
Rediscover the power of praise
Laugh with them
Defend the boundaries
Recognize the uniqueness in each child
Set yourself free from what other people think
Empathise with the things that matter to them

Don't ever give up
Finally... let them go.

Setting yourself free from what other people think is possibly the hardest of these ten to achieve. We are moulded by our cultures all over the world and it takes brave people to go against the social mores of their day, what should be done instead of what you actually want to do. My son Jens made the choice to leave university. He tried it and it hasn't suited him and he is now exploring new directions in life. It takes courage to walk in a different direction.

I only regret the things I didn't do when I could, that is, when I was fit and physically more able than I am now. So my advice is do whatever you can while you can and do your best to fulfill those hopes, dreams and ambitions.

Several people I know have stopped putting off doing something they really wanted to do, or stopped putting off not going to somewhere they really wanted to go to. They said it was because of me and they call it: *The Gilly Factor*.

The suddenness with which life can change, as I said to Lisa at the beginning of this book. But I think of people taken out by car accidents who never had the chance to say goodbye. I have discovered new things to do but most of all spending time with those whom I love, my husband, my children, my wider family and my friends. I was aware of it before my diagnosis but it took my diagnosis to bring it into sharp focus.

I used to wonder what had caused my tumour. My mum thinks it was a fall from a horse when I was young; I used to think it was stress and anxiety, worrying too much, but it was probably none of those things. None of the medical experts know.

In fact one of my children asked the Spanish consultant who originally diagnosed me what had caused it. He swung around in his swivel chair and said, 'If I knew the answer to that question I would be a millionaire'. I view my tumour as my destiny, in other words no one's fault, except my genes' maybe. Caroline, my sister, who is a biology teacher, says with the complex processes all cells have to go through, it's a miracle any come through healthy and intact. Life is a miracle,

I agree. Treasure every day.

9

LETTERS TO THE CHILDREN

*The greatest thing you'll ever learn is
to just to love and be loved in return.*

David Bowie

I hadn't been able to buy the children their Christmas presents because I was rushed into hospital so I decided to write them each a letter instead. I gave them these on Christmas Day.

A message from Mum

To Cal

You set an exceptionally, wonderfully high standard and example as our first born – from your initial deep look at your world around you to your intelligence, care and compassion as your younger siblings joined you, your sense of calm and perspective and all of these qualities mixed with a tremendous, fresh and quick sense of fun – it made the dynamic of the four of you a joy to see as you grew up with each other together.

With your steady guidance your younger siblings have been nurtured so well into the dynamics of family life. You have been generous in doing this – it could have been so different so I feel deeply proud of your attitude at the position you found yourself placed as eldest.

I am in awe of your mind and how you see things and come so succinctly to a point after quietly observing. I have listened and waited for your viewpoint more than you know – and often wait to hear what you think or feel before I trust something to think or do myself. You handle yourself with dignity and a calm inner strength that is inspiring to be around.

I loved watching you grow from my first born baby to my first born motivated, talented, moral, and wise young man – It's inspiring how you see things – artistically, professionally, personally, socially and about us as a family, your friends and the wider world.

You have been a complete joy to me to have and then to have been able to share with you so many precious and lovely, fulfilling, rich years together; to have seen you develop and bring you up through all your life. You'll be hugely successful in business in a lovely, decent, moral way and show such integrity and honesty with your fellow business colleagues – you deserve great success because you nurture goodness and see potential in people and encourage them using your innate sense of excellent leadership which is a big talent you have. Thank you for being the most wonderful first born. You have been an inspiration. Now also keep having fun, as I love your sharp wit so much. I love you. x

To Kitty
You're our daughter who was so very wanted and waited for – your birth was a euphoric shining light day in my life – and that deep feeling has remained every single moment, since I first saw your very tiny delicate feline features and

called you Kitty. The pride and joy I felt at you, my own beautiful little girl in my arms, permeated through me all through your sparkly, fun childhood and has lasted every single day since then as you have grown into a wonderful, sensitive and wise young woman.

Every time I look at you I simply can't get over how utterly beautiful you are, both physically and in spirit. In your inner being – you have such beauty of spirit. You are a constant source of happiness, sparkle and wisdom all bubbling together in your every day way attitude to everything life throws at you. You are a loyal daughter who gives your love to us all generously.

How did someone as heavenly as you come from me is a question that has foxed me much! You have such amazing humour – and with that your extraordinary talent for communication – putting people at their ease, warm and funny and intelligent at the same time. My daughter who brought to me the joy and camaraderie, the shared secrets and giggles of the feminine side of things, surrounded as we were by all our boys.

You light up the room when you walk in and the light stays shining for as long as you are in the room. And that's the feeling I've had inside me from the day you were born. You will be unquestionably, gracefully successful in both your private and business life – so many people want you to be part of their lives and you generously give them your time and loyalty. They flock, personally and in business life to you and want to share with you your talents and happiness. Keep having fun in both - my talented, positive, humourous, wise, loyal, generous, thoughtful soul mate daughter. Thank you for being all those things to me and such a truly wonderful daughter. And bringing pink and glitter into my life!

I love you. x

To Jens

Jens – my large bundle of compassion, you who sat for the first few years of your life like a wise Buddha serenely, beatifically observing us all. You have added immeasurably to our family and we all rely on your fantastically quirky observations on us, our lives and the world. When you aren't there to add your voice we all try to guess what you would do or say – and yet somehow we know we can't get it right without you because you are too unique. And you make us laugh and laugh more with your humour and choices and questions.

You, who always 'got' my quirky moods, and seem to innately, sensitively understand how people are feeling. Your compassionate nature and incredible people and observation skills are your exceptional talent - At the highest standard - and you are very loved by so many for possessing this unique gift. Use it all your life Jens – you will anyway, it's completely natural to you. You will be successful in your business life in a way that will hold a candle up as to how it should be done in human terms – and the world needs a bit of that. And your smile, oh that smile of yours, so unique, I have watched endless people melt in its warmth. I melt in its warmth.

So constantly and generously given by you to us and to the world whatever it throws at you; your smile that lights up peoples lives and has also done so for me since your very first smile. There's something about you and your smile together that says the world is a much better, gentler, peaceful place if we could all look at it and see it from your perspective - and I and our family have loved being part of your perspective. The best thing is when others see it too. And how you now, as you have grown into a beautiful young man, also add just the right thing to say to people that makes them walk on air and feel special. Oh – and you know how to have lovely, joyous, easy, fun too and there's a talent keeping just that right balance there and you do it with style!

I love you. x

To Robin

Ah, our little late lamb –who completed our family for me. You have had to speed down sand dunes literally and metaphorically since joining us.

Your wise, beautiful, calm physical features as a baby and strong intelligent eyes observed us all carefully as you then found your own very special place in your siblings dynamics. Your arrival pulled us all very close together as a family - you provided a new focus for your siblings to care and nurture the core of our family as you fitted yourself in so comfortably to their relationships and their individual characters. You then began contributing your own strong and unique perspectives on their conversations, so much younger and yet in a wise and measured manner that made them listen and take account of your views.

So you have grown up beyond your years, partly because you had to with your position in the family – but also because you chose to listen and do this well and motivate yourself for all these adventures ahead that you heard about and saw. This personal choice you made to embrace all the conversations and plans around you has nurtured your development, your soul and perspective on the world in an incredibly inspiring way – and that's your talent, making such a wise choice in the first instances and developing yourself to the very best you can be.

I have loved being stretched intellectually by you. Your powerful sense of justice, morals, care and deep compassion for the underdog and what is the right thing to do – your deeply held moral code on the injustices in the wider world and protection for your dear sharks, your extraordinarily wide and deep and exploration and questioning of esoteric ideas and subjects has inspired and challenged me and nourished my soul in our discussions. And you also know exactly how to have fun and a laugh and be completely down to earth as well and look cool which is a rare and incredible combination! You portray such dignity in attitude. There is no question you are going to be successful– and may even do your part to change the world in some way for a better place – maybe save a species. You have the passion, motivation, morals, intelligence and tenacity to succeed. Have fun doing it too.

I love you. x

So finally…

I feel such completeness with you four – because all four of you bring your own unique something to the world and each of you make it better place in your own way. What an achievement! How did I do that?… Aha! It wasn't just me… I can't hog all the credit; just half… which brings me to your Dad…

To Christian
The person I fell so completely instantly in love with. You were doing an upside down somersault into the snow and I knew. That was it. No one else, ever, forever. I didn't even know your name! And thirty-three years later I still feel the same. No one else could even come close to the depth of love and respect I feel for Chrish my Dish, who has had to manage, nurture and guide my foibles, my eclectic and vivid imagination and plans and dreams.

You have been our very centre rock – always providing financially for us – but so incredibly much more than that with a very deep, straight, powerful, moral sense of what family is and should be. So you have unfailingly given us constant protective love for our family that has made me feel very safe through all these years.

Through the ups and downs of our years together – the stuff of life and marriage – you have never doubted me, I have never doubted you and we always pulled back together – as close as we began. Through you I truly do believe it is in our human kind to find one partner for life –and how lucky I have been that I did. It has been my greatest achievement along with the four children we then created! Actually I think the achievement is the greater on your part because you have held us all and particularly me so steady.

You have the deepest, compassionate business moral ethics and ways of treating your colleagues and employees that is a shining light – and should be held up as a template to make the business world such a better, less confrontational world. Your honesty, respect, care and compassionate and the way you communicate with anyone from the people regarded as the very lowest by others in the working world to the very top and everyone in between is unfailingly equal – and I see the joy in so many people for being given that respect. You see it as respect for each human that should be unquestionably given. So many can't even begin to grasp that concept. It was something I fell even more in love with about you as we began to go out. You spoke to everyone and took an interest in all of them equally, not above or below – and that brings out the best in people. What a gift.

And gosh do you know how to have fun!....and shared that with me. Joy of life and humour and good friends and crazy laughs that have coloured our time together with such brilliant memories and laughter and warmth.

And haven't we danced. – The best person to dance my way through life has been you – is you – will be you. We will never stop dancing together in my heart.

I love you – absolutely. Thank you.

So .....all of you. Look after each other, I know you all will.

And haven't we had the most fantastic laughs and fun on our family journey – keep having lots more.

10
CAROL4ACURE

Exactly one year after my diagnosis, on December 10 2015, we held a charity Nativity event, Carol4aCure. It was organized by my son, Cal, with the help of Kitty, Jens and Robin and involved all their friends putting on a nativity play and an evening of carols and Christmas songs. It was a sell-out with four hundred tickets sold. The Brain Tumour Charity was there.

The evening was a great success, raising over £26,000 for research into brain tumours, the most left behind, least researched, of all cancers. Brain tumours are often particularly difficult to diagnose in children where death rates are the highest of all cancers. It is still one of the least known about, least funded and least curable cancers. It is growing at a somewhat alarming rate and so much more research needs to be done, along with huge needs for costly new diagnosis machinery.

It was a great evening, with a nativity play that was fun but not irreverent, a cheeky boys dance that was balanced by a demure girls dance!

This was my speech given at the beginning of the evening after the opening Carol, Once in Royal David's City.

My Carol4aCure Speech

On this date last year I woke really happy and excited because it was my first official day representing a film company, Knew Productions, and I was really keen to do my best.

But I thought I had an ear infection, so I decided to quickly nip into the doctor, ask for some antibiotics and pop them down, so I could crack on in top form and not let my new employer, Richard, down. The appointment was at eight thirty in the morning. Within twenty minutes I was in a paramedic ambulance and my life, as I knew it, flipped, so suddenly and so completely.

The shock and the fear of my immediate diagnosis, an aggressive malignant brain tumour, stage 4 and incurable - was the start of a different life and a new world.

From the very first doctor, to my neurosurgeon, Mr. Rupert Price, to every nurse, including my Macmillan nurses, to the young tea boy who remembered I liked ginger biscuits and smuggled them into me in his pockets, to the night nurses working through the long hours of the night, when we patients are often at our most distressed, to the Croatian anaesthetist who gave up his precious day off just before Christmas to bicycle to work for my operation... just so that I may have a chance to get home for Christmas... every one of them – and all of you here have made so many of my fears, not just bearable but amazingly, a privilege, in the insights I have been given through this last year into human kindness, generosity and love, dedication and expertise, compassion and our shared humanity.

The deep comfort, support and importance of my family – immediate and wider; the flow of love and prayers from friends – so many of you here tonight – to me and us as a family – has been constant and humbling. I have never felt that I'm fighting a lonely battle – so thank you, from my family and me.

In this bleakness there have been some funny moments. Once, at the hospital, I got mixed up with another lady. My family later told me that before I emerged from the lift after five hours of brain surgery, they had been waiting by the wrong lift. Suddenly, a tiny, very old, white-haired lady was wheeled out. *Good God*, they all thought, *what has the surgeon done to Mum?* I was then wheeled out of the adjacent lift to find my family with that nervous laughter you get in heightened situations.

There was also the occasion when as the family and I drove down the drive to go to hospital I made two requests. 'Please don't forget to pick up the turkey I've ordered' and 'Please don't forget to put the bins out'. Which one do you think they remembered?

Cal was promoted to chief Santa and with his three elves the four children went and did all the Christmas shopping in a very grey, cold and rainy Stoke-on-Trent, while I was in hospital. When they arrived back at the ward they all looked like they were the ones who needed brain surgery especially Jens who had just arrived back from sunny Miami and was still in his swimming trunks.

I know people wonder how I was feeling as I walked into my neurological ward at North Staffordshire University Hospital for major brain surgery. The truth is, there's always someone worse off – the first thing I saw was a young, very sick, teenage boy – with his parents watching over him. No child, I thought, should ever have to go through this.

As I lay in hospital over the next few days, listening to Christmas carols, all about a baby born in very difficult circumstances, but yet who brought hope to the world and engendered the generosity of kings, I thought: *every new life brings hope*.

So tonight brings together the celebration of the hope that a new baby born over 2000 years ago brought to the world and in the support you are all giving to be here this evening, huge hope to all those who are told, that they or their child has this little understood and frightening diagnosis.

I have been so lucky to have Christian by my side. His unfailing and constant love and support has made this year less tough for me…but very tough for him. Thank you.

I'm now fighting to defy the grim statistics I'm up against but all year I've looked for and found silver linings and tonight is a big one.

Thank you.

Epilogue

My desert island discs! I never made the show!

Out of Africa theme from the film, John Barry
Clarinet concerto in A, Adagio. Wolfgang Amadeus Mozart
'You're just too good to be true' - Andy Williams
'If only for one night' and 'Get Here' - Brenda Russell
'Peace on earth' - David Bowie and Frank Sinatra
'Viva la Vida' - Coldplay
'Djobi Djoba' - Gypsy Kings
'Walking on Sunshine' - Katrina and the Waves
'Cinema Paradiso' - Ennio Morricone
Vivaldi, Winter of Four Seasons - by the group Bond
'Close to you' - The Carpenters
'I vow to thee my country' - Beck Goldsmith version
'Song Bird' - Eva Cassidy

Book: The largest of anthologies of poetry ever published.
Must include Rupert Brooke and Emily Dickinson.

Then I have music and poetry... divine nourishment for
my free-flying soul.

Favourite plays:
The 2013 Royal Shakespeare Company version of *Peter Pan and Wendy* at Stratford
Accidental Death of an Anarchist - Dario Fo
Noises Off - Michael Frayn
Steel Magnolias - Robert Harling

Favourite musicals:

Cabaret - from a novel by Christopher Isherwood with music by John Kander and lyrics by Fred Ebb

The Lion King - from the Walt Disney film, directed by Julie Taymor, music by Elton John, lyrics by Tim Rice

Miss Saigon - by Claude-Michel Schonberg and Alain Boublil

Favourite statue:
La Pieta in the Vatican by Michelangelo

Favourite authors:
Kuki Gallman, Amanda Fuller - for how they write about Africa
Paul Gallico
C.S.Lewis
Noel Streatfield
Roald Dahl
John Mortimer

Favourite artist: Camille Pissaro
Favourite painting: 'Girl with a Twig' - Camille Pissarro

Favourite films:
Cinema Paradiso
Moulin Rouge
Out of Africa
Notting Hill
Four Weddings and a Funeral
The Sound of Music
Robin Hood, Prince of Thieves
Witness
Crocodile Dundee

Gallipoli
Life is Beautiful
The Cassandra Crossing
Pretty Woman
Arthur
Oceans 11
Local Hero
Born Free
Life of Others
Dear Frankie
Narnia
Crash
Whale Rider
Billy Elliot
Shadowlands
An Officer and a Gentleman
Philomena
Lion

My sister, Jacky, is a quilter and she made the most beautiful quilt for me. It is different coloured petals around a central golden circle. I love the way quilts tell stories. She wrote this story to go with the quilt:

Life is like a flower with petals of many colours. Each petal represents a chapter in our lives. Each colour, and therefore petal, will bring a new experience and new feeling to you.

Today you have picked a dark petal, but tomorrow you will pick a new petal of a bright and cheerful colour that will bring new energies back into your colourful being.

At the centre is the golden core, vibrantly shining as the anchor and support to each petal.

The golden centre represents your family and true friends who are always there to provide the anchor, strength and support you need to pick the next petal in the chapter of life.

I dedicate this garden of colour quilt to you today and just know I am with you in the centre every step along the way.

The Whitchurch Little Theatre Group fed my desire for a creative outlet. I joined one year after moving up to Cheshire when the children were really small (1994) As well as being huge fun and stimulating, I made many close friends in the local community. I wrote 'Catwalk', a three-act play, and then directed it. It was received very well. There are too many people to mention but Derek and Jennie Harrison were at the centre of the group and often directed me: my favourite plays were 'Noises Off' (I played Brooke) directed by Derek and 'Calendar Girls' (I played Annie) directed by Jennie. I miss it all and the people so much but I am now not physically able to move around a stage freely or learn lines. So I hold on to the warm, happy memories and evenings filled with a lot of laughter and really good friendships. I will be eternally grateful they gave me the chance to play the part of Peter Pan. Thank you all of you in the group for giving me such happy times!

With thanks to everyone for all the help with lifts, meals, gardening and care of Baloo. We were given holidays and for all the books I was given to read to help me through chemotherapy. In particular:

Ray and Belinda Bailey, Jackie Bourne, Shelley Brookes and family, Caroline Brown, James Budd, Henry (Gap Year Buddy) Lucy and Holly Clark, Helen Clarke, Alison Dodwell Cooke, Carol Cope, Honey Denny, Belinda Diamond, Janie and Robert Farquharson, Kit Farmer, Caroline Fishbourne, Matt and Jo Gomez, Kate Halewood, Jeremy and Nix Helsby, Wilf and Debs Helsby, Rachael Hill, Sharma Jamieson, Jojo Jones, Mark and Becky Johnson, Helen Langley, Lisa Law, Denis and Sheila Lee, Pia and Heidi East-Lee, Vanessa Lee, Christine Lomax, Richard and Margaret Knew, Neil and Rosie Lamont, Philly Kitchin, Chris Mortimer, Emma O'Keeffe, Steve and Jane Parker, Tim and Carole Saunders, Erica Sears, Nikky Shergold, Caroline Socha, Philly Stewart, Amanda Stothert, The Whitchurch Little Group, Carolyn Ware, Sarah Webster, Mark and Kirsty Williams, Fray and Mandy White, Isobel Williamson, Jill Wiseman.

And of course my sisters, Cecelia, Jacky, and Caroline, and my mother and father for all their love and support and care.

Thanks to Rachael Hill, Caroline Socha, Christian Lee, Sharma Jamieson and Jacky Arkell for reading through it and encouraging me. And to the four children for contributing their own words so readily.

My huge thanks to my publisher James Essinger of The Conrad Press for his help with revising and editing this book, and all his encouragement, and to Charlotte Mouncey for designing the cover and typesetting the book. Charlotte's website address is www.bookstyle.co.uk

And finally to James's tadpoles in his garden pond, who, I believe, all have tiny little individual souls.